BAD' AL-AMALI

AQIDAH ~ SERIES

Bad' al-Amāli

English Translation of a Classical Text on Sunni Creed

IMAM ÁLĪ IBN ÚTHMĀN AL-ŪSHĪ
(d. 575 AH / 1179 CE)

Translated by
ABU HASAN

RIDAWI
PRESS

Manżūmah Bad'il Amālī

By

Imam Sirājuddīn Álī ibn Úthmān al-Farghānī al-Ūshī

Translation and Footnotes
Abu Hasan

Acknowledgements
Abu Nibras, **Aqdas**, **Noori**, **Janab Aqib Farid Qadiri**, **Ubaydullah**, **Sayyid Ali Khalid**, **Esfak**, **Abu Hanifah** and all others who contributed to this book.

Special thanks to **Mufti Zahid Husain** (Preston) for reviewing the drafts.

Cover: Mohammed Imtiyaz

Muĥarram 1439 / October 2017
Version 1.2

First Version Released in August 2017 (Dhu'l Ĥijjah 1438)

Published on Amazon by
Taftazani Press

feedback@ridawipress.org
copyright@ridawipress.org
complaints@ridawipress.org
admin@ridawipress.org

The translator can be contacted at:
abu.hasan@ridawipress.org

CONTENTS

بِسْمِ ٱللَّهِ ٱلرَّحْمَٰنِ ٱلرَّحِيمِ

الحمد لله واجب الوجود والصلوة والسلام على أكمل مظاهر الحق في مرأى الخلق نبي الرحمة وشفيع الأمة
وعلى آله وأصحابه الطيبين الطاهرين

TRANSLATOR'S PREFACE

All praise be to Allāh ﷻ the Creator and Sustainer of all creation. Blessings and peace be upon our master Muĥammad ﷺ, the chief of all the Prophets and Messengers; our master was sent with guidance and as a guide to the world. O Allāh! We ask Thee to guide us towards truth and upon the right path.

Every Muslim should learn the fundamentals of faith [*áqīdah*], which is also termed as obligatory knowledge. There are many short and lengthy works on this subject and this poem on Sunni creed [*qaşīdah*] is well-known and used to be a component of elementary education in the past.

This *qaşīdah* is written by Imām Álī al-Ūshī, a Ĥanafī scholar who lived in the 6th century of the Islamic calendar. He was born or lived in Uūsh, by the Farghana valley (Osh in today's Kyrgyzstan) and hence his demonym al-Ūshī.

The present translation of *Bad' al-Amālī* is intended to be a beginner's guide and a handy reference of the Creed of Ahl al-Sunnah. A transliteration is appended in the end, as an aid to students who wish to memorise the poem. A few footnotes (such as the one on *takwīn*) are more technical and lengthier than they ought to be in a book for beginners; however, they were necessary for a better understanding of the couplets in question.

Many thanks to brothers who reviewed the translation and made valuable suggestions and corrections. A special thanks to Mufti Zahid Husain Qādirī of Preston, for his review, suggestions and corrections. I had started this translation in 2014 as a quick project, but had it shelved due to other commitments. I began working on it again, late last year and I felt that some explanatory notes would make the text more accessible to beginners and to those without an introduction to *kalām*. By the Grace of Allāh táālā, the translation was completed in February 2017, but it could not be released until now for various reasons. I hope and pray to Allāh táālā to make this book a useful resource for students, and grant acceptance to this small service, and include it in my record of good deeds, and to forgive me, my parents, my family and my friends.

نسأل الله العافية

Abu Hasan

3rd Dhu'l Ĥijjah 1438 / 25th August 2017

BAD' AL-AMĀLĪ

1. Says the slave[1] in the beginning of his dictation –
   On Tawĥīd;[2] a string of pearls, its composition.

2. The God of Creation,[3] our Lord,[4] is pre-eternal[5]
   He can be attributed [only] with Attributes of Perfection.[6]

3. He is the Living, the Absolute Planner[7] of everything;
   He is the Real;[8] the Ordainer of everything,[9] the Glorious.[10]

---

[1] By *ábd*, the author refers to himself; i.e. slave of Allāh ﷻ.

[2] *Tawĥīd*: Monotheism – and by extension, the Islamic faith, even though there are other religions that claim to be monotheistic; in our terminology this refers to the belief of Muslims and everything that entails, which can be described in one sentence as 'Obedience to Allāh ﷻ and His Messenger ﷺ.'

[3] *Ilāh al-Khalq*: One who is worthy of worship, *mábūd*.

[4] *Mawlānā*: Commonly, this is used as an honorific or a title to address men of learning; here, it is used in the sense of: 'our Absolute Master'. Just as *ĥakīm* is used to mean a physician or a wise man; and *ĥakīm* referring to Allāh ﷻ means 'the Wise'.

[5] *Qadīm*: He exists without a beginning and there was nothing in Pre-eternity with Him; everything was created by Him; everything else is therefore *hādith,* which means that it 'occurred' or that it came into existence and was previously non-existent.

[6] *Şifāt;* Allāh ﷻ cannot be attributed with flaws. For instance, falsehood is a flaw; therefore, Allāh ﷻ cannot be attributed with falsehood. The Mútazilah believed that it was possible for Allāh ﷻ to lie. Some modern sects are attempting to revive this heresy. *Al-íyādhu billāh.*

[7] *Ĥayy*: Living; and it is unlike 'life' of anyone in the creation. *Mudabbir*: He who Plans.

[8] *Ĥaqq*: The Absolute Reality.

[9] *Muqaddir*: He has Destined everything for everybody. We believe in destiny and that everything is ordained by Allāh ﷻ.

[10] *Dhu'l Jalāl*: The Glorious; He who is attributed with Absolute Majesty.

4. He Wills [to Create] both the good and the ugly evil;
But He is not Pleased with [sin and] transgression.[11]

5. The Attributes of Allāh are not His Self[12] per se;
Neither are they separate, nor are they dissociated.[13]

6. All His Attributes of Self and Attributes of Action,[14]
Are pre-eternal, and are free from annihilation.[15]

---

[11] *Muhāl*: literally, it means 'impossible'; here, it is used to mean transgression [Qārī]. The good or evil [or its ugliness] is known by revelation; the Mútazilah say that it can be known rationally; they also say that the good is from Allāh ﷻ but evil is man's own doing. We say: Indeed, evil is manifest by human actions and is a consequence of exercising their free-will; but still, it is created by Allāh ﷻ. ***He is not Pleased for His slaves to disbelieve*** [Zumar 39:7].

[12] *Dhāt* = Essence, Self.

[13] The Mútazilah say that His Attributes are His Self and there is no difference; the Karrāmiyyah say that they are separate and distinct from His Self. But we say that His Attributes are neither Self nor separate from Self. For example, Allāh is Merciful, and Mercy is His Attribute; but Allah and His Mercy are not one and the same thing. Neither is His Mercy, His Essence in itself, nor is it a separate entity dissociated from the Essence. Therefore, clichés such as 'God is love' or 'God is Power' are unislamic and absurd.

[14] *Ṣifāt al-Dhāt* = Attributes of His Self; those attributes whose opposites are impossible for Allāh ﷻ. For example, Knowledge is an Attribute of Essence; its opposite is ignorance. Another attribute is Greatness [*kibriyā'a*] and it is impossible to attribute its opposite to Allāh ﷻ. Similarly, Divine Power, Hearing, Seeing and Divine Will are *ṣifāt al-dhāt*.

Ṣifāt al-Fiýl = Attributes of Action; those attributes whose opposites can also be attributed to Allāh ﷻ. For example, *iĥyā'a* is to give life; its opposite is *imātah*, taking away of life (or giving death). It is true that Allāh ﷻ gives life and death; it is permissible to attribute Him with both the opposing attributes [of giving life and giving death]. Such attributes are known as *ṣifāt al-fiýl*.

[15] All His Attributes are pre-eternal, without a beginning, and Everlasting, without an end. Māturīdīs consider all the attributes of Allāh ﷻ as pre-eternal – thus, He was *Rāziq* [Giver of Sustenance] in pre-eternity, when none existed to whom He could give sustenance. He was *Khāliq* [Creator] even when He had not created anything. The Ashárīs, say that *ṣifāt al-dhāt* are pre-eternal, but *ṣifāt al-fiýl* are accidents [*ĥādith*]. This is only a semantic difference and not a major point of contention. Also discussed in distich #50 below.

7. We say, Allāh is an Entity,[16] unlike any other entity;
He[17] is transcendent of all the six directions.[18]

8. The 'name' is not dissociated from the named[19]
According to the people of discerning, the virtuous ones.[20]

---

[16] *Shayy*: Entity, something that exists. Due to linguistic constraints, we use the word *shayy* or 'entity' to describe 'existence' or 'He who exists' [*mawjūd*]; but it is absolutely unlike anything else, whether in Essence or Attributes. In other words, He Exists and He is unlike everything else. The Jahmiyyah sect claims that it is not permissible to describe Allāh ﷻ as *shayy*, i.e. as an Entity [Qārī]. In the Qur'ān, ***Ask them: 'Whose witness is the greatest?' Say: Allāh is the [greatest] Witness between I and you*** [Anáām, 6:19]. In the above verse is the word, *ayyu shayy*; literally, 'which thing' [translated as 'whose'].

[17] *Dhāt*: His Self. It is permissible to use the word *dhāt*, or Self or Essence for Allāh ﷻ as said in the ĥadīth: ***lā tatafakkarū fī dhāti'llāh*** [Do not ponder in the Essence of Allāh ﷻ, or in His Self]

[18] The six directions are - above, below, front, back, right and left. Allāh ﷻ is transcendent of being in ANY direction. The Creator is transcendent of time, space and direction; these are constraints and are attributes of the creation. The Karrāmiyyah said that Allāh ﷻ can be attributed with [any of] the six directions. Furthermore, this is also a refutation of the Mútazilah, who say that Allāh ﷻ is present in 'every place' [*fī kulli makān*]; the anthropomorphists and Karrāmiyyah also say that He is 'upon' the Throne [*ársh*]. We seek Allāh's refuge from describing Him in a manner that is suggestive of anthropomorphism.

[19] The Jahmiyyah, Karrāmiyyah and Mútazilah say that the name, in itself, is a distinct entity. They cite the phrase, 'the name of your Lord' as an example, and say, 'if both were one and the same, why would they be mentioned separately? When one says 'fire', the tongue does not get burnt - that thing which burns is removed and is distinct from the name. Therefore the name and the entity are two separate things. This is the argument of the aforementioned sects. According to the Ahl al-Sunnah: The name and the named are one and the same. When one says, 'Zaynab is divorced', it is Zaynab herself who is divorced, not the name. In the verse, ***Glorify the Name of your Lord*** [Al-Aálā, 87:1] - the praise and glorification is for Allāh ﷻ Himself - not for a name separate from Him. Qāđī Bayđāwī said in his tafsīr: The 'name', when used as a 'word' [*lafż*], is separate from the entity; but the 'name', if it refers to the essence of the named [*dhāt*], then they are one and the same. Ibn Jamāáh said that his teacher found it strange that people argued about this non-issue.

[20] Refers to the Ahl al-Sunnah.

9. My Lord Sustainer is not an atom[21] or a body[22]
Neither [described as] whole, nor a part, nor constituted.[23]

10. My son, it is rational to accept the existence of a particle –
With the attribute that it cannot be divided any further.[24]

---

[21] *Jawhar* = particle, substance, matter; *jawhar al-fard* = indivisible particle, or the atom. The property of a substance is that it occupies space and has a position [*taĥayyuz*]. *Árad* means an accident, an occurrence. The difference is that *jawhar* exists in itself; *árad* occurs because of an extraneous cause and *árad* cannot exist by itself.

[22] *Jism* = body, composed of parts, particles. It is composed of particles which occupy space, and is described in terms of height, length and depth. A body can refer to a living or non-living thing – anything that occupies space and has a position is a body. The Karrāmiyyah and the anthropomorphists [*mushabbihah*] say that Allāh ﷻ is 'a body unlike other bodies'. The Ahl al-Sunnah say that Allāh is not a substance, or a particle, neither a body nor an accident [not a *jawhar* or a *jism* or an *árad*].

[23] *Kull* = all, completely; this indicates composition of parts or particles. It is impermissible to describe Allāh ﷻ as 'all' or a 'portion' or a 'part' or that He is composed of 'parts' or 'portions', because these terms imply space and position, which are attributes of creation.

[24] The theologians [*mutakallimin*] among Ahl al-Sunnah favoured the theory that it is reasonable to imagine the existence of an **indivisible particle** [*jawhar al-fard* or *juz' al-ladhī lā yatajazza'*], even though it may not be observed externally, as it may be attached to other [such particles], which they described as *nuqţah,* or a 'point'. This was mentioned by Qārī in the 16th century CE. Even today, sub-atomic particles hypothesised by physicists and known as protons and neutrons cannot be observed directly; physicists say that their presence is inferred or presumed by indirect observation and detected by traces in particle accelerators. If a person denies the existence of sub-atomic particles just because he/she cannot see them, they will be ridiculed as ignorant and foolish. Glory be to Allāh! How can one deny a Creator just because they cannot see Him with their eyes? The whole universe, the numerous intricate and complex systems are all 'evolved', according to believers of Scientism. They make exceedingly absurd arguments in their attempts to disprove the existence of God and make fun of those who believe in a Creator. One should not be intimidated by the clamour of atheists or fear ridicule of peers for believing in a Creator.

Often, atheists say, 'show us God' or 'why doesn't God do this or that' or 'why is the state of the world thus' etc. The Qur'ān tells us about such people and their destination: ***And***

disbelievers will never cease doubting, until the Final Hour comes upon them suddenly, or comes punishment, on that day which will be fruitless for them [Ĥajj 22:55]. Such objections are not new, and similar arguments have been made in the past, as mentioned in the Qur'ān.

When Sayyidunā Mūsā ؑ took seventy Israelites [*banū isrāyīl*] along with him, they dissented and said: ***We will not believe you until we see Allāh openly [with our own eyes]*** [Baqarah, 2:55]. In the time of the Prophet ﷺ, the Jews and Christians asked him to produce a book descending from heaven, to believe in him ﷺ; Allāh ﷻ says: ***The People of the Book ask you to cause a book to descend upon them from the heavens. They have asked Mūsā for something even greater than this, when they said: 'Show us Allāh manifestly.' They were struck by a thunderbolt for their transgression.*** [Nisā'a, 4:153].

When reminded of death and afterlife, disbelievers scoff at it: ***When our signs [Qur'ānic verses] are recited to them, they say: 'These are naught, but legends of ancient folk'*** [Qalam, 68:15]. When reminded of life after death, they dismiss it: ***Indeed, there is nothing else except our death for just once; and we shall not be resurrected. Bring forth our forefathers if you are indeed truthful.*** [Dukhān, 44:35-36]. When warned of an eternal punishment, they laugh at it: ***When he comes to know of our signs [Qur'ānic verses] he takes to mockery...*** [Jāthiyah, 45:9]. But death is sure to come: ***Death will come to you, even if you take shelter in the most formidable fortress...***[Nisā'a, 4:78]. They will continue to disbelieve and mock believers ***Until death comes to them, and they will say: 'O our Lord, send us back'*** [Mu'minūn, 23:99]. But it will be too late. ***If only you could see the Angels yank the souls of disbelievers, and slap their faces and strike their backs, [saying:] 'Now, taste the punishment of the scorching fire'*** [Anfāl, 8:50]. Until then, ***Be lenient with disbelievers and give them some time.*** [Ţāriq, 86:17]. Tell those who do not believe to do as they like, and leave us Muslims to do what we deem to be good deeds; as for punishment for disbelief, tell them: ***Do wait; indeed, we too are waiting.*** [Hūd, 11:122].

In summary, Sunni scholars held that it is rational to accept the existence of a fundamental particle that has a position [occupies space, howsoever infinitesimal] and which cannot be subdivided further. Ancient philosophers and some factions among the Mútazilah [such as followers of Nażżām] believed that it is impossible for such an indivisible particle to exist, and that every particle can be subdivided infinitely. According to Mawlānā Álī al-Qārī, this is not a matter of Islamic creed, but information that is only good to know. Rayĥāwī, however, is of the opinion that this issue has important implications in various creedal matters. Allāh táālā knows best.

11. The Qur'an[25] is not the creation of Allāh; Exalted is
The Speech of my Lord Sustainer from being an utterance.[26]

---

[25] The word, *Qur'ān,* has different meanings:

1. Recitation or reading out something [*qirā'ah*]
2. The Book [*muṣ'ĥaf*] or a written/printed copy of the Qur'ān
3. Divine Speech, which is uncreated and is a pre-eternal Attribute of Allāh ﷻ, also known as *Kalām Nafsī.*

Here, the author refers to the third meaning, i.e. Divine Speech. Therefore, scholars cautiously say, 'the Divine Speech of Allāh' is uncreated [*kalām Allāh ghayr makhlūq*] and do not say 'the Qur'ān is not creation' [*al-qur'ānu ghayr makhlūq*] to avoid confusion, lest people are misled to believe that the written word, the sounds and letters, the recitation of the Qur'ān are all uncreated and pre-eternal. It is obvious that neither our voices, nor the sounds we make, nor the letters made with ink on paper are pre-eternal. Some Ĥanbalī scholars made weird statements that defy common sense; for example, a Ĥanbalī said [see *Musāmarah* of Ibn Humām]: "The Divine Speech of Allāh is composed of letters and sounds and subsists by His Self"; another said: "the binding and the cover of the book [in which Qur'ān is written] are also pre-eternal". We ask Allāh ﷻ to protect us from deviance.

[26] Uttered speech is made of letters and sounds; and these are attributes of the speech of creation. Exalted is the Divine Speech of Allāh from being similar to attributes of creation or resembling the uttered speech of creation.

The Qur'ān is Divine Speech of Allāh ﷻ which was revealed to the Prophet ﷺ, written in books, recited upon tongues, memorised and preserved in the hearts – but it does not mean that Divine Speech has entered or blended into any of these created things. The sounds and letters, and that which is written, recited and memorised is a denotation, an indication and expression of Divine Speech. The information in Divine Speech is conveyed via sounds and letters due to constraints of human faculties. For more details, see my upcoming paper *Kalām Nafsī-Kalām Lafżī*. Whoever says that the Qur'ān – as in Divine Speech – is created, is a kāfir.

A man asked Imām Aĥmad ibn Ĥanbal ؓ: "Can I pray behind a person who drinks wine?" He replied: "No." The man asked "Can I pray behind a person who says that the Qur'ān is created?" Imām Aĥmad said: "SubĥānAllāh! I forbade you to pray behind a Muslim, and you are asking me about a kāfir?"

12. The Lord of the Throne is on[27] the Throne,[28] but –
Sans the attribute of being situated upon it or in contact.[29]

---

[27] *Fawq* = on, upon, above; the word should have been *istawā'a/istiwā'a*, but replaced with *fawq* due to poetical necessity. However, *fawq* is also mentioned in the Qur'ān: ***And He is Omnipotent over His slaves*** [Sūrah Anáām, 6:18]. *Istiwā'a*, as mentioned in the Qur'ān: ***Raĥmān made istiwā'a on the Throne*** [Sūrah Ṭā-Hā, 20:5]. The literal translation of *istiwā'a* is equability, to become equal, to be on the same level; it has other figurative meanings such as subduing, overcoming etc. The real meaning is only known to Allāh ﷻ. Later scholars permitted explaining such that it does not contradict the established creed of Ahl al-Sunnah.

[28] *Ársh* = Throne.

[29] Being upon it physically, seated upon it, 'established' upon it [*tammakun*] or being in contact [*ittiṣāl*], are all attributes of creation and impossible for Allāh ﷻ. The Karrāmiyyah, the anthropomorphists and the Shīáh say that the Throne is His seat, and its meaning is literal. We say that the Throne was created to Manifest His Greatness and to show His Immense Power upon creation – not because He is in any need of it, for Allāh ﷻ is transcendent of being in need of anything. *Istiwā'a* means subduing [*Bakri*]. Imām Mālik was once asked about its meaning and he replied: "[That Allāh made] *istiwā'a* is established; its quiddity is not known; to investigate its meaning is heresy; and to believe in it is obligatory." [*Qārī*]. On the other extreme, the Jahmiyyah deny *istiwā'a* as a Divine Attribute. The Ahl al-Sunnah tread the moderate path; we do not deny Divine Attributes as the Muáṭṭilah and Jahmiyyah or interpret them literally like the Ĥashwiyyah.

Ibn Humam says in his *Musāyarah* [p18]: **The Eighth Principle** –Allāh ﷻ made *istiwā'a* upon the Throne, by His Divine Command. *Istiwā'a* does not mean seating or settling of a body upon another body; *istiwā'a* does not mean being placed, or touching, or being in contact, or being in proximity etc. [*tamakkun, mumāsah, muĥādhāh*]. Rather, its real meaning is known only to Allāh ﷻ. In summary: It is obligatory to have faith that Allāh ﷻ made *istiwā'a* upon the Throne and at the same time [it is obligatory to] negate anything that suggests anthropomorphic ideas or implies similitude to creation. It is permissible to explain *istiwā'a* as 'subduing' or 'exercising dominion' [*istīylā'a*], as it is contingent and subject to Divine Will. Since we cannot know Divine Will [except when He Himself informs us], it is a valid possibility; though, it is only obligatory for us to believe in *istiwā'a* itself [and not required to know its meaning]. If the absence of an explanation would cause confusion [to common people], who may then imagine it to be an attribute of a body, it is better to steer them towards an explanation away from anthropomorphic ideas; besides, explaining it as 'overpowering dominion' is consistent with linguistic interpretation.

13. There is no similitude for Raĥmān[30] in any aspect[31]
Protect yourself by agreeing with virtuous company.[32]

---

[30] Raĥmān is among the exclusive names of Allāh ﷻ – and those names belong to Allāh ﷻ alone. Ignorant people truncate compound names and address people as 'Raĥmān'; this is impermissible. Just as Ábd-Allāh [slave of Allāh] cannot be truncated to 'Allāh', Mr. Ábd al-Raĥmān ['slave of Raĥmān'] or Mr. Ĥabīb al-Raĥmān ['beloved of Raĥmān'] should not be truncated to Mr. Rahman. *al-íyādhu billāh.*

[31] The author has used the word *wajh* – which means aspect, and also face or countenance, hinting that *wajh,* as mentioned in Qur'ān has no similitude. Anthropomorphists translate this word literally, whereas it is impermissible to attribute its literal meaning to the Lord Almighty, and impossible for Him: ***Wheresoever you turn, you will find the Mercy of Allāh facing you*** [Baqarah, 2:115]. It is also mentioned in 2:272, 13:22, 18:28, 28:88, 30:38-39, 55:27, 92:20. Allāh ﷻ does not resemble anything in His creation in any manner; neither in His Self, nor in His Attributes. ***There is nothing like Him*** [Shūrā, 42:11].

[32] The scholars of Ahl al-Sunnah repudiate any similitude for the Creator and believe in the transcendence of the Creator [*tanzīh*]. Ibn Humām says in Musāyarah [p18-19]: "Things mentioned in the Qur'ān and reported in Şaĥīĥ ĥadīth whose literal meaning has connotations of being a body, such as finger [*işbá*], foot [*qadam*], hand [*yad*] etc. – it is obligatory to believe in them [even if one does not agree with the interpretation] because the *yad* or *işbá* are Attributes of Allāh, not as a body part, but in a manner that is befitting His Exalted Majesty, and [the real meaning of] which is known only to Him. Thus, *yad* and *işbá* are explained as His Divine Power and Absolute Dominion; *yamīn* [lit. right hand] mentioned in the ĥadīth of RasūlAllāh ﷺ for the Black Stone [*ĥajar*] is indicative of the honour and greatness accorded to it. These explanations are in consideration of the intellects of commonfolk and to help them steer clear from concepts of anthropomorphism. These explanations are only possible meanings – we do not insist that they are the exact meanings. Our scholars have said that these are abstruse verses [*mutashābihāt*] and no one can know their real meanings in this world." Blind followers of Ibn Taymiyyah often translate *wajh* as 'face' and *yad* as 'hand' in English, and scoff at Sunnis for translating them as 'His Self' or 'His Power'. The fools do not realise that translating *yad* is, in effect, an interpretation. Anthropomorphists writing in Arabic seek refuge in the pretext: 'Thus it is mentioned in the Qur'ān'; their non-Arab counterparts do not understand this nuance, and happily strut around advertising deplorable translations [which are actually interpretations], and disgusting anthropomorphist beliefs. Exalted is Allāh ﷻ from such descriptions attributed to Him سُبْحَانَهُ وَتَعَالَىٰ by ignoramuses and evil folk.

14. Al-Dayyān[33] [Allāh ﷻ] is transcendent of time,[34]
Exalted is He from [constraints of] period[35] or state.[36]

15. The Lord God is transcendent[37] of having wives;[38]
Or children – whether male or female.[39]

16. So also, He is not in need of any helper or supporter,
He is Alone in His Absolute Majesty and Greatness.

---

[33] *Dayyān* is derived from *dīn*, which means recompense. Allāh ﷻ has said: ***The Lord of the Day of Recompense.*** [Fātiĥah, 1:4]. It is one of His Divine Names as mentioned in hadith: *Allāh ﷻ will gather all the people; and they will be summoned by a voice they will all hear: 'I am the Absolute King, I am the Giver of Recompense'* [Bukhārī, introduction to the ĥadīth #7481]. In another ĥadīth: *The good shall not perish; the sin will not be forgotten and Dayyān does not die. Be as you wish, you will be recompensed for whatever you do.* [*Maqāşid al-Ĥasanah*, #834, Sakhāwī from Aĥmad in *Zuhd*, Daylamī, Abū Nuáym etc].

[34] *Waqt* – time. Allāh ﷻ is the Creator of time and is not constrained by it. He exists independent of space and time.

[35] *Zamān* – period, epoch, point in time such as past, present or future. The *before* and *after* are not applicable to the Attributes of Allāh ﷻ.

[36] *Hāl* – state. That is, the state of a thing changes over time. For example, after birth, as time passes, one's state changes from childhood to adolescence to youth to middle-age and then old-age. Allāh ﷻ is transcendent of time; He does not change. He is, as He always was; and shall be, as He has always been.

[37] *Mustaghnī* – lit. independent, free from; Allāh ﷻ does not need a wife or children; He is Absolutely Independent from having any. It is *muĥāl* [impossible] for Allāh ﷻ to have an equal, or a partner, or a wife, or children – be it sons or daughters.

[38] *Nisā'a* – lit. women; however, it is intended to mean wives and is repudiated in the Qur'ānic verse: ***And that Exalted is our Lord Sustainer; He has not taken [unto himself] a wife or a son.*** [Jinn 72:3].

[39] Christians claim that Jesus ﷺ is the son of Allāh ﷻ; the polytheists of Makkah used to believe that angels were the daughters of Allāh ﷻ. Exalted is He from such ascriptions – for He is Absolutely Alone; neither does He have children, nor is He born of anyone; nor does He have any equal, or a partner, or a rival.

17. He gives death to creation by His Power,[40] then resurrects;
And gives them recompense according to their deeds.[41]

---

[40] *Qahr* – He subjugates by His Infinite Power. He has ordained death for every living thing, as He has said: ***Every soul shall taste death***. [Aāl Ímrān, 3:185].

[41] The Horn shall be blown twice by the angel Isrāfīl ﷺ. At the Final Hour, it will be blown for the first time, and everything existing and everyone alive until that time will perish, including the angel blowing the Horn. Then a period of time will pass when everything in the creation will be annihilated and will cease to exist [*mádūm*]. Allāh ﷻ will ask: ***Whose dominion is it this day?*** As there will be none to answer, He will Himself reply: [*Everything*] ***belongs to Allāh, the One, the Absolute Subduer*** [Ghāfir, 40:16]. Thereafter, Allāh ﷻ will resurrect the angel Isrāfīl, who will blow the Horn for the second time. Everyone will then rise from the dead; this is known as *nashr* or Resurrection. It is also said that some beings will not be exterminated at the first blowing of the Horn. It is mentioned in ĥadīth that the period between the two Horns is 'forty'. Abū Hurayrah ؓ, the narrator of this ĥadīth, was asked whether it was forty days, months or years; but he declined to confirm. It is obligatory for a Muslim to believe, that sending forth from the graves towards the Assembly [*baáth*], the Gathering [*ĥashr*] and the Resurrection [*nashr*] are all true. Every living thing will be gathered after having decayed and turned to bones and dust. However, the bodies of Prophets, martyrs and Awliyā'a-Allāh will not decay and their bodies will remain untouched even after their deaths. Also, Prophets are alive in their graves, after the inevitable moment of death, as every soul is bound to taste death. Allāh ﷻ will resurrect all the bodies and return their souls on Judgement day; and it is these renewed bodies which will be assembled, not merely the souls, as claimed by some philosophers. Some among the Karrāmiyyah claimed that bodies will not be recreated; philosophers have entirely rejected the belief that bodies will be resurrected. Atheists reject afterlife and according to them death is the end of everything. This is not a new belief and the Qur'ān quotes ancient folk who have said similar things: ***There is nothing else except for our life in this world, we die and we live; and we shall not be resurrected.*** [Mu'minūn, 23:37]. They believe that it is just time that ravages them; ***And they say, there is nothing [else] except this life of ours in this world; we die and we live and it is only time that wastes us away. They do not speak from knowledge – it is merely their conjecture*** [Jāthiyah, 45:24]. This couplet in *Amālī* is a summary of the Qur'ānic verse: ***Every soul shall taste death. You will be given your full recompense only on the Day of Resurrection. Whosoever is saved from Fire and made to enter Paradise [on that day] has truly succeeded. The life of this world is nothing but a materialistic delusion*** [Aāl Ímrān, 3:185].

18. For the good,[42] there is paradise and luxury;[43]
And disbelievers will suffer[44] a painful torment.[45]

---

[42] Only Muslims will enter paradise and righteous Muslims will enter paradise without going through hell. Some sinners among Muslims will go to hell and after being punished for a period, they will be removed from hell and sent to paradise after the intercession of RasūlAllāh ﷺ. It is also true that some sinners will enter paradise upon the intercession of RasūlAllāh ﷺ, without going through hell. Perennialists believe that Islām is not necessary for salvation and that regardless of religion, people will go to Heaven. The prominent figure of *Sophia Perennis* in our time is Seyyed Hossein Nasr, a disciple of Frithjof Schuon. Nasr and his students have tried to promote their philosophy and attempted to tamper with the Qur'ān, by sneaking far fetched extrapolations in a spurious work titled, *The Study Quran*, published by Harper Collins. Muslims are warned to keep away from this devilish design to subvert Islām and misguide unsuspecting and ignorant folk. Such attempts will never succeed anyway, as Allāh ﷻ has Promised to Safeguard the Qur'ān from alteration and manipulation. ***Indeed, We have revealed this Qur'ān and We shall Protect it***. [Ĥijr 15:9]. We belong to Him ﷻ and towards Him ﷻ is our return.

[43] Paradise is a place of unmitigated luxury and unending comfort. There are vast gardens and palaces for those who enter it. There will be no fear of disease, or hardship, or grief, or oppression, or affliction, or suffering or any sort of discomfort. There will be no danger, or crime, or misfortune, or injury, or death. Everybody who enters paradise will be young and beautiful and will live therein forever. There will be streams of milk, honey, pure water and pure wine flowing in these gardens. Pebbles and gravel will be made of diamonds and pearls, the bricks will be made of gold, and mortar will be of pure musk. Nobody will have to toil or work for anything – if one desires something, it will be presented immediately for their enjoyment and to their satisfaction. Everyone in paradise will be similar to a thirty-three year old youth in perfect health and vigour. Only a few things that we can understand and imagine are mentioned in the Qur'ān and ĥadīth – otherwise, there are things therein that no eye hath ever seen, no ear hath ever heard, nor has its thought crossed human mind. The Qur'ān says: ***No soul knoweth what is hidden for them, among things extremely pleasing to the eyes, as a reward of their deeds*** [Sajdah, 32:17].

[44] *Darak* means to suffer or endure; *durk* [rhymes with murk] is the deepest level in hell, as said in the Qur'ān: ***Indeed, the hypocrites are in the lowest depths of hellfire*** [Nisā'a, 4:145].

[45] Even though some sinful Muslims will enter Hellfire, they will not stay there forever. See distich #62 further below for more information.

19. Neither Hell, nor Paradise will ever be annihilated[46]
Nor will the dwellers of these two abodes be removed.[47]

20. Believers will see Allāh ﷻ without modality[48]
Not by perception[49] of the senses, or in similitude.

21. When they see Him, they will forget every other blessing
Alas! What a great loss for the Mútazilah[50] on that day!

---

[46] The Najjāriyyah, Jahmiyyah and Mútazilah claim that Heaven and Hell will eventually be destroyed. The Qur'ān says that the disbelievers will live in Hell forever: ***Indeed Allāh has damned the disbelievers and has prepared for them a blaze. They shall stay in it forever*** [Aĥzāb 33:64-65].

[47] After the last person among sinful Muslims [sent to Hell] is taken out from Hell and made to enter paradise, death will be brought in the form of a ram and slaughtered. After this, none of the dwellers of Heaven or Hell will leave their abodes. They will live in thier places forever and ever after, as mentioned in the ĥadīth: *After the [last] of the entrants to Paradise enter it, and the last of the people of Hell will go to Hell, Death will be brought forth and slaughtered between Heaven and Hell and an announcer will proclaim: 'O people of Heaven, dwell therein forever and there shall be no death; and O people of Hell, suffer therein forever for there shall be no death.' [Upon this,] the joy of the people of Heaven will multiply and the agony of the people of Hell will amplify.* [*Bukhārī* #6548, *Muslim* #2850].

[48] The Najjāriyyah say that Vision [*ru'yah*] of Allāh is a vision perceived by the heart; the Karrāmiyyah say that Allāh ﷻ will be seen as a body [we seek Allāh's refuge]. The Khawārij, Zaydīs among Shīáh and Mútazilah say that it is impossible to see Allāh ﷻ. The Ahl al-Sunnah say that believers will see Allāh ﷻ with their eyes, but without modality.

[49] *Idrāk* – to see something that the sight can encompass; that which can be bounded by sight. Muslims will see Allāh ﷻ without modality or similitude – not facing Him, not in a place, or in any direction or in any form; nor will the sight encompass Him. The seeing of Allāh ﷻ shall be the greatest reward for believers.

[50] In general, all those who deny the possibility of seeing Allāh ﷻ will feel sorry on that day for their heretical belief. Qārī says that it indicates that Mútazilah may be deprived of the vision, even if they enter Paradise, because of their stubborn refusal to accept the many ĥadīth that mention seeing Allāh ﷻ in Paradise.

22. Doing that which is best [for us], is never an obligation[51]
Upon the Absolute Guide,[52] the Glorious, the Exalted.

23. It is obligatory[53] and compulsory to accept all Messengers[54]
And the honourable Angels; they, of immense grace.[55]

---

[51] *Wujūb al-Salāĥ w'al-Aṣlaĥ* – According to the Mútazilah, it is obligatory upon Allāh to do what is good or best for His slaves. We, the Ahl al-Sunnah, say that nothing is obligatory upon Allāh ﷻ; He can choose to do or forgo what He Wills. Further, there are two factions within Mútazilah on this issue: One group says that it is obligatory in all matters; the other group says that it is only obligatory in religious matters. Concerning what is meant by 'choosing the good/best': The first faction says: It means that which agrees with [common] wisdom. The second faction says: It means whatever is [more] beneficial for us. [Summarised from *Tuĥfah* of Bājūrī, gloss on *Jawharah*, distich #51].

[52] *Hādī* has two meanings: the Creator of guidance and He who guides [the act of guiding]. ***He lets go astray whom He wills, and He guides whom he Wills*** [Naĥl, 16:93].

[53] It is obligatory upon every person and is a necessary tenet of Islām to accept and believe in all the Prophets عَلَيْهِمُ السَّلَامُ. Denial of even one Prophet is *kufr*. Similarly, considering someone a Prophet when the Sharīáh does not sanction him/her as a prophet is also *kufr* – such as those who have claimed, or will claim to be prophets after the coming of our Prophet ﷺ. Our Prophet ﷺ is the last of all Prophets and Messengers and any claim of prophethood after his advent is undoubtedly false and invalid.

[54] Also includes Prophets, even if only Messengers are mentioned in this line. Prophets [*nabiy, anbiyā'a*] are humans who receive Revelation [*waĥy*] even if they are not commanded to deliver the message; but Messengers [*rasūl, rusul*] are Prophets who are commanded to deliver the Divine Message to people and to invite them towards Islām.

[55] It is obligatory to believe in Angels, who are ethereal and luminous beings. Allāh ﷻ has created them from light. Among angels mentioned in the Qur'ān by the name are: the Archangel **Jibrīl; Mīkāyīl** [or **Mīkāl**]; **Mālik,** who is the Chief Keeper of Hell. The names **Isrāfīl** and **Riđwān**, the Chief Guardian of Paradise are found in ĥadīth; The Chief Angel of Death is mentioned in the Qur'ān but not named; he is commonly known as **Ízrāyīl,** from other sources such as Jewish traditions. Other Angels are mentioned in the Qur'ān and ĥadīth, but it is not clear whether these are their proper names or whether they are categories of Angels: The Bearers of the Throne [*ĥamalat al-ársh*], Guardian Angels [*ĥafażah*] also **Kirāman-Kātibīn** [the Scribes of Good and Bad Deeds], the angels of death

24. The Seal of Messengers[56] at the forefront[57] of pre-eminence[58]
The Prophet from the Hāshimī[59] clan; the most handsome.[60]

25. He is the leader of all Prophets,[61] without contention
The Crown of the elect, the immaculate[62] without a doubt.

[the assistants of **Ízrāyīl**], the **Zabāniyyah** [Angels of Hell], **Khazanah** [keepers of Heaven and Hell], **Mudabbirāt al-Ámr** [The Planners and Dispensers of Commands] and **Munkar-Nakīr** [Inquisitors in the Grave]. See Imām Jalāluddīn Suyūṭī's book *Al-Ĥabāyik fi Akhbāri'l Malāyik*, for a detailed exposition of this topic.

[56] Our Master, Prophet Muĥammad ﷺ is the last of all Prophets and Messengers – the Seal of Prophets as mentioned in the Qur'ān: ***Rather, he is the Messenger of Allāh and he is the Seal of all Prophets*** [Aĥzāb, 33:40] and in the ĥadīth: *Prophethood ends with me* [*Muslim*, #523], and *There is no Prophet after me* [*Muslim*, #2345].

[57] Qārī says that the word 'forefront' [*ṣadr*], is used to indicate that he ﷺ was the first of all Messengers to come into existence [*awwalu'r rusulī wujūdan*], even though he ﷺ is the last to appear among people, as said in the ĥadīth: *I was a Prophet when Ādam* ﷺ *was still a body without soul.* In another ĥadīth: *I was the first among Prophets to be created and the last to be sent forth [baáth].*

[58] Our Prophet ﷺ holds the highest rank among all Prophets and Messengers, as explained in the next distich. This greatness will be witnessed by everyone on Judgement day when our Master ﷺ will be the first to speak and the first whose intercession will be accepted.

[59] The Hāshimī clan was the most respectable and prominent among the Quraysh.

[60] *Dhī Jamāl* – literally, it means handsome; indeed, RasūlAllāh ﷺ was exceedingly beautiful and exceptionally handsome; yet, here it is used figuratively to mean that he was a paragon of mercy and kindness as mentioned in the Qur'ān: ***We have not sent thee, except as a mercy to the universe.*** [Anbiyā'a, 21:107].

[61] In the ĥadīth: *I will be the leader of all the children of Ādam on the Day of Judgement. The Standard of Praise [liwā'a al-ĥamd] will be in my hand on that day – and I say this without pride. There will not be a Prophet on that day – whether Ādam or anyone else, except that they will be under my Standard. I will be the first for whom the earth will be opened [and will come out of the grave] and [I say this] without pride.* [Tirmidhī, #3615].

[62] *Aṣfiyā'a* are those whom Allāh ﷻ has chosen [*ṣafwatullāh*], such as Prophets and the Awliyā'a Allāh, His friends. Or it is from *ṣafī* meaning the immaculate, spotless and chaste.

26. His Sharīáh shall remain valid at all times
Until the Final Day, and the End of the World.[63]

27. The Ascension[64] is real; it is true and validated –
There is evidence from reliable and authentic reports.[65]

RasūlAllāh ﷺ among the righteous folk is like the crown – the most precious, the most honoured and the most esteemed.

[63] His Sharīáh – or Law – abrogates the laws of all previous Prophets such as Sayyidunā Ibrāhīm, Sayyidunā Mūsā and Sayyidunā Ýīsā ﷺ. This Divine Law shall be binding upon all until the Final Day – because RasūlAllāh ﷺ is the last Prophet and no other Messenger or Prophet will ever come after him. The second coming of Sayyidunā Ýīsā ﷺ is not the same as the coming of a new Prophet after RasūlAllāh ﷺ. See distich #32 for more details.

The Jahmiyyah say that the Sharīáh of RasūlAllāh ﷺ will completely end or will be partially rescinded at the second coming of Sayyidunā Ýīsā ﷺ; but according to the Ahl al-Sunnah, when he returns, Sayyidunā Ýīsā ﷺ will follow and rule according to the Sharīáh of our Master RasūlAllāh ﷺ. He shall be the deputy [*khalīfah*] of RasūlAllāh ﷺ as mentioned in the ĥadīth: *Then Ýīsā, the son of Maryam ﷺ, will come from the west; he will validate the truth of Muĥammad ﷺ and will be his follower* [Imām Aĥmad in his *Musnad* from Samurah ibn Jundub]. Even if he receives revelation [*waĥy*], it will be concerning other matters and not the Sharīáh, as it is said in the ĥadīth in *Şaĥīĥ Muslim* [#2937] concerning Gog and Magog, that Allāh ﷻ will command Sayyidunā Ýīsā ﷺ to take the people to the top of a hill.

[64] *Miýraj* – the Ascension of RasūlAllāh ﷺ to the heavens and beyond. The Night Journey is *Al-Isrā'a* as mentioned in the Qur'ān: ***Glory to Him, who took His slave on a journey from the Masjid al-Ĥarām to the Farthest Mosque [Masjid al-Aqşā, Jerusalem] in a portion of the night...*** [Al-Isrā'a, 17:1] Whoever denies the *isrā'a* or the Night Journey, is a disbeliever; however, those who deny *miýrāj* or the Heavenly Ascension are heretics and not disbelievers. We believe that the Prophet's ﷺ Night Journey was physical, in a wakeful state and not a dream; and from Jeruṣalem, he ascended to the heavens and beyond. He ﷺ also saw Allāh ﷻ with his own eyes, in a wakeful state; this is the opinion of Sayyidunā Ábdullāh ibn Ábbās ﷺ and is favoured by the majority of Sunni scholars. Some scholars, however, say that his seeing Allāh ﷻ was with his blessed heart and not with his eyes, based on the opinion of our mother, Sayyidah Áayishah ﷺ.

[65] There are numerous reports about this well-known miracle. The ĥadīth that describe this miracle are well-known and accepted by successive generations of scholars.

28. It is hoped that intercession[66] by People of Virtue,[67] will benefit
Sinners, with enormous sins,[68] big as mountains.[69]

29. Verily, Prophets are protected, they are immune[70]
From committing sins deliberately; or from being deposed.[71]

---

[66] In addition to Prophets and Messengers عَلَيۡهِمۡ ٱلسَّلَامُ, martyrs, saints, scholars and many others will intercede for sinners on Judgement Day, by the leave of Allāh táālā.

[67] Prophets and Messengers عَلَيۡهِمۡ ٱلسَّلَامُ. RasūlAllāh ﷺ has said: *My intercession is for those in my nation who have committed enormities* [Qārī].

[68] Enormities, *kabāyir* or the Deadly Sins; Taftāzānī mentions the following in his commentary on *Nasafī's Creed*: polytheism, murder, accusing a chaste woman of adultery, adultery, abandoning the battlefield, sorcery, embezzlement of an orphan's property/wealth, mistreating and disobeying Muslim parents, committing a sin [major or minor] in the Sanctuary [Ĥaram], usury, stealing, drinking wine. There are still more sins considered as *kabāyir* in Islām, such as eating pork, illicit sexual relations [adultery, fornication], homosexuality, omitting obligatory prayers, etc. Imam Dhahabi has listed enormities in his short work titled *Al-Kabāyir*. Ibn Ĥajar al-Haytami has also compiled a two-volume work on this topic named *Al-Zawājir án Iqtirāf al-Kabāyir*. Also, any of the *kabāyir* or enormous sins can be forgiven except polytheism and other forms of disbelief.

[69] This distich is repeated in #58, and omitted in some commentaries.

[70] *Íşmah, máşūm*: We believe that Prophets are Divinely Protected from committing sins, deliberately or inadvertently, whether enormities or minor sins. By common agreement, it is impossible for Prophets to commit enormities both before and after their prophethood; also, it is impossible for them to commit minor sins which are base, vile or despicable such as cheating, lying, etc. However, a group of Sunni scholars say that it is possible for them to commit a minor sin inadvertently [*sahw*]. Nevertheless, concerning our Prophet ﷺ, there is a unanimous agreement among all the Islamic sects, that he ﷺ is immune from sins – whether major or minor, or committing sins deliberately or inadvertently.

[71] It is impossible for Prophets to be deposed from their rank of prophethood; they are Divinely Protected from being dispossessed of their prophethood. Qādī Bayđāwī says: 'If Prophets could commit sin, they would become oppressors and then they would be deserving of being dismissed from prophethood' [*Maţāliý* p.215]; hence the author's inclusion of 'dismissal' alongside the mention of immunity from committing sins.

30. Never has a female[72] been a Prophet –
Or a slave; and neither a liar, nor a vile character.[73]

31. Dhu'l Qarnayn[74] is not known to be a Prophet and –
So also Luqmān;[75] desist arguing about it.[76]

---

[72] All the Prophets [*nabiy*] are humans and are males; but Messengers can be either humans or angels. The majority of scholars opine that being a male is a condition for prophethood. Some scholars such as Imām Abu'l Ĥasan al-Asharī and Qurţubī say that it is possible for a female to be a prophet. This contention is about six noble ladies mentioned in the Qur'ān: Maryam [Virgin Mary, the mother of Sayyidunā Ýīsā عليه السلام], Aāsiyah [Pharoah's wife], Sārah, Hājar, the mother of Sayyidunā Mūsā عليه السلام [Yūĥānidh or Miĥyānah or Bārkhā] and Ĥawwā'a [Eve, the mother of all humans and the wife of Sayyidunā Ādam عليه السلام]. In the Qur'ān: ***And We have not sent forth [a Messenger] before you, except men*** [Anbiyā'a, 21:7].

[73] All Prophets are free men, of noble character and of high birth. Also, prophethood is not given to liars, sorcerers, soothsayers or to men of despicable traits.

[74] *Dhu'l Qarnayn* – He of the Two Horns. He was a righteous Muslim king who travelled from the east to the west and is mentioned in the Qur'ān. According to the predominant opinion, Dhu'l Qarnayn and Luqman are not prophets; Tubbá and Khađīr are also debated upon. One should not insist or claim certitude concerning either opinion. The Greek Alexander was a disbeliever and contemporary of Aristotle. The other Alexander [*Sikandar*] was a Roman-Muslim and a contemporary of Khađir [Khiđir or Khiđar]; the Alexander/Dhu'l-Qarnayn mentioned in the Qur'ān is the latter.

One should not specify an exact number for Prophets and Messengers, even though it is mentioned in a weak ĥadīth: '*Indeed, the number of Prophets is 124,000; and 315 among them are Messengers.*' [Imām Aĥmad in his *Musnad* #22288 from Abū Umāmah رضي الله عنه].

The following are the names of twenty-six Prophets mentioned in the Qur'ān: Our masters – Ādam [Adam], Nūĥ [Noah], Ibrāhīm [Abraham], Isṁāýīl [Ishmael], Is'ĥāq [Isaac], Yáqūb [Jacob], Yūsuf [Joseph], Mūsā [Moses], Hārūn [Aaron], Shuáyb, Lūţ [Lot], Hūd, Dāwūd [David], Sulaymān [Solomon], Ayyūb [Job], Zakariyyah [Zechariah], Yaĥyā [John], Ýīsā [Jesus], Ilyās [Elijah], Yasá [Isaiah], Yūnus [Jonas], Idrīs [Enoch], Dhu'l Kifl [Ezekiel], Şāliĥ, Úzayr عَلَيْهِمُ السَّلَام and our master Muĥammad عَلَيْهِ وَعَلَىٰ آلِهِ الصَّلَاةُ وَالسَّلَام.

[75] Luqmān the Wise is mentioned in the Qur'ān, but he is not considered a Prophet.

[76] We do not say they are Prophets, but if someone claims they are prophets we do not quarrel with them [Bakrī].

32. Ýīsā 🕮 will return presently, and thereafter slay[77]
Dajjāl,[78] the false messiah, the evil reprobate.

33. Miracles[79] of saints [*Awliyā'a Allāh*], in this world
Have a basis, and they are the benevolent folk.[80]

---

[77] It is obligatory to believe that Sayyidunā Ýīsā 🕮 will return to earth shortly before the final hour. This will be his second coming and he will lead Muslim armies against the antichrist and kill him [*dajjāl*].

[78] Literally, *dajjāl* means a big liar, a deceiver, an impostor. It refers to the antichrist who shall appear in the end times and claim to be a god. He will display feats that defy nature that are deemed impossible; he will acquire a horde of followers. After his descent from the heavens, Sayyidunā Ýīsā 🕮 will slay him. It is also mentioned in the ḥadīth [*Bukhārī* #7121] that nearly thirty other lesser-Dajjāls will appear, and every one of them will claim to be a prophet of Allāh, even though our Master 🕮 is the Seal of all Prophets and there shall be no prophet after him 🕮. In the 19th century CE, a man named Ghulām Aḥmad of Qadian claimed to be a prophet – his followers are known as Qadiyānīs, though they call themselves as 'Ahmadi Muslims'. RasūlAllāh 🕮 has informed us about Dajjāl and the signs to identify him. Dajjāl will be a man of white complexion, heavily built, very hairy and will have curly hair; he will be blind in one eye. It is also said, that his other eye will be green. Other major signs of Tribulation are: the sun will rise from the west, a Terrene Beast [*dābbatu'l arḍ*] will appear, Gog and Magog will emerge and Mahdī will appear. Many minor signs will also occur prior to the major ones: ignorance will be prevalent, the number of scholars will dwindle and knowledge will decline; confusion and strife will be widespread; mindless killing will become common, Muslims will imitate Jews and Christians in everything, even trifling matters; dishonesty will be rife and many Muslims will become apostates; shamelessness and adultery will become rampant, homosexuality will be commonplace and gay marriages will be deemed normal. In a ḥadīth it is mentioned that 'people will vie with one another to propose marriage to a young boy, just as one of you would propose to a virgin girl'.

[79] We believe that miracles – supernatural occurrences, i.e. events that defy nature – are possible. The Khawārij and Mútazilah do not believe in miracles.

[80] *Waliy, Awliyā'a* are Friends of Allāh, or saints; they are people who have attained gnosis of the Attributes of Allāh and will be scrupulous in obeying the commands of Allāh; they will be extremely cautious and wary of committing sins. A *waliy* will have overcome his/her base desires; they will be abstemious and abstinent from worldly pleasures; he/she will be

34. A *waliy* is never considered superior, anytime,[81]
To a Prophet or a Messenger – despite such claims.[82]

35. Şiddīq[83] is given precedence, superiority and prominence
Upon all the Companions, without any exception.[84]

---

eager to do good deeds and worship, and will be anxious about success in the Hereafter. Such a person is constantly busy in the remembrance [*dhikr*] of Allāh and does not hanker after wealth, fame and glory. Saints reach high stations by being obedient to Allāh and His Messenger ﷺ. They will never consider themselves free from the bounds of Sharīáh; a person who claims to be unrestrained by Sharīáh, and claims exemption from obligatory actions such as prayer and fasting is an outright heretic and an apostate.

[81] It is impossible for a saint or *waliy* to be superior to Prophets or Messengers, even if that saint/waliy/imām is from the Blessed Household [*ahl al-bayt*]. In fact, one Prophet alone is superior to all the saints and imāms combined. It is kufr to believe that a non-prophet is superior to prophets. Some among the Karrāmiyyah sect say that it is possible for saints to become superior to Prophets; it is a common belief among the Twelver Rāfiḍīs that the imāms of Ahl al-Bayt are superior to all the previous Prophets, as mentioned in Khomeini's *Velayat e Faqeeh* [p.35, Translated into English by Hamid Algar, ©Iran Chamber Society]:

> "It is one of the essential beliefs of our Shī'i school that no one can attain the spiritual status of the Imams, not even the cherubim or the prophets."

[82] Whether one claims such superiority for himself or for others, it is unfounded. One can do good deeds and be pious and be elevated to the rank of a *waliy*; but prophethood is not 'earned' by any means –Allāh ﷻ grants it to whom He wills: ***Allāh Knows well, whither to place His Message*** [Anáām, 6:124].

[83] Sayyidunā Abū Bakr al-Şiddīq ؓ. His name is Ábdullāh ibn Úthmān Abi Quĥāfah. He was the first man to accept Islām. The Prophet ﷺ named him *Şiddīq*, meaning the Truthful and the Affirmer of Truth. Bakrī says in his commentary: "Whoever says that someone else [i.e. non-prophet] is superior to Abū Bakr al-Şiddīq, is either a Mútazilī or a Rāfiḍī. They curse Abū Bakr ؓ and Úmar ؓ and dissociate themselves from all the companions except Álī ؓ, and thus plunge into heresy." He was born two years after RasūlAllāh ﷺ, and passed away two years after the passing of RasūlAllāh ﷺ. He is buried by the side of RasūlAllāh ﷺ in Madīnah al-Munawwarah.

[84] Including Mawlā Álī ؓ; the *Tafḍīliyyah* sect does not curse or revile Abū Bakr and Úmar, nor denies their caliphate, but claims that Mawlā Álī is superior to both. Scholars have said that even if it is a minor aberration, it is the doorway to the major heresy of Rāfiḍīs.

36. Fārūq[85] has a distinct precedence and superiority
    Over Úthmān, Bestowed with Two Sublime Lights.

37. The One Bestowed with Two Lights[86] is certainly superior
    To the Unflinching Stalwart[87] in the ranks of battle.

38. [Álī], the Unyielding Warrior[88] has superiority thereafter
    Upon everyone else,[89] without exception; be at ease.

---

[85] Sayyidunā Úmar ibn al-Khaṭṭāb al-Fārūq ⁕. RasūlAllāh ⁕ gave him the title *al-Fārūq* – the Discerner between Truth and Falsehood [Nawawī]. He was born 13 years after the Raid of the Elephants [the year of RasūlAllāh's ⁕ birth]. He accepted Islam in the 6th year of proclamation, at the age of 27. He became the Khalīfah after Abu Bakr ⁕ in the year 13 AH. He was martyred at the age of 63, in the year 23 AH by Abū Lu'luah, a Persian slave. He is buried near the feet of Abū Bakr ⁕ in the mausoleum of RasūlAllāh ⁕.

[86] Sayyidunā Úthmān ibn Áffān Dhu'n Nūrayn ⁕ was born 6 years after the Elephant Raid. He was among the earliest Muslims and among those who migrated twice: first, to Abyssinia and then to Madīnah. His mother Arwā was RasūlAllāh's ⁕ cousin. He was a wealthy trader, and he readily spent his money for the welfare of Muslims and the cause of Islam. Úthmān was first married to Sayyidah Ruqayyah ⁕, RasūlAllāh's ⁕ daughter, who passed away on the very day the news of victory at Badr [3 AH] reached Madīnah. Thereafter, he married Umm Kulthūm ⁕, the third daughter of RasūlAllāh ⁕. He earned the appellation: 'He, Bestowed with Two Lights' as he married two daughters [lights] of RasūlAllāh ⁕. He became the Khalīfah in 23 AH after Úmar ⁕ was martyred. His period was marked with tumults and unrest. He was martyred by rebels in the year 35 AH, at the age of 82. The collection of the Qur'ān in a standardised script was completed in his time.

[87] *Ḥaydar al-Karrār*; i.e. Sayyidunā Álī ibn Abu Ṭālib ⁕.

[88] Sayyidunā Álī ibn Abu Ṭālib, Abū Turāb Abu'l Ḥasan ⁕. He was RasūlAllāh's ⁕ cousin and the first among children to become Muslim. RasūlAllāh ⁕ gave his youngest daughter, Sayyidah Fāṭimah in marriage to Sayyidunā Álī ⁕. The Prophet ⁕ was given Revelation on Monday, and Álī ⁕ accepted Islam the next day. He was only 7 or 10 years old when he accepted Islam. He is known as the 'Lion of Allāh' for his bravery in battle. He became the Khalīfah after Úthmān ⁕ was martyred. A faction of fanatical extremists broke away from his troops at Ṣiffīn, and are therefore called The Deserters [*Khawārij, Khārijite*]; Ibn Muljam, a Khārijite, martyred Mawlā Álī ⁕ in the year 40 AH.

[89] Meaning the rest of the companions and those who came after them. The four rightly guided caliphs [*khulafā rāshidūn*] are deemed superior in the order of their *khilāfah*. In

39. The Şiddīqah[90] has precedence, and know this –
Over the blessed flower, Zahrā'a[91] in some attributes.

40. Yazīd is not cursed after his death,
Except by a person holding an extremist view.[92]

---

addition to the four, six others were given glad tidings of paradise, and they are: Zubayr ibn al-Áwwām, Saád ibn Abī Waqqāş, Ábdu'r Rahmān ibn Áwf, Ţalĥah ibn Úbaydullāh, Saýīd ibn Zayd and Abū Úbaydah Áāmir ibn al-Jarrāĥ رضي الله عنهم. We must respect all the companions, because RasūlAllāh ﷺ has warned against disparaging his companions. We should not discuss the disputes, disagreements and the wars that occurred between them or judge their actions and intentions. In the battles that took place among the companions, Mawlā Álī رضي الله عنه was in the right; others were mistaken in their judgement. Imām Shāfiýī رحمه الله reports that Úmar ibn Ábd al-Ázīz رحمه الله said: 'Allāh ﷻ has protected my hands from being stained in their blood; I do not wish to stain my tongue by disparaging them'.

[90] Our mother, Sayyidah Áayishah Şiddīqah رضي الله عنها is the daughter of Abū Bakr al-Şiddīq رضي الله عنه. One group of scholars consider her to be the most superior among all women, because of her exceptional intelligence, the breadth and depth of her knowledge and the fact that she was the most beloved wife of RasūlAllāh ﷺ. In a ĥadīth, when a companion asked RasūlAllāh ﷺ, which person was most beloved to him, he replied: 'Áayishah' and when the companion said: 'Among men?' he replied: 'Her father'. [Bukhārī, #3662]. When she was falsely accused by hypocrites of being unchaste, the Qur'ān vindicated her and proclaimed that she was chaste and unblemished. The Rāfiđīs, in their mindless hate, slander her; anyone who accuses our spotless and virtuous mother of being unchaste is a kāfir – may the damnation of Allāh be upon such a vile creature. The Mother of Believers, Sayyidah Áayishah رضي الله عنها passed away in the year 58 AH in Madīnah.

[91] The noble lady, Sayyidah Fāţimah رضي الله عنها was the dearest to RasūlAllāh ﷺ among his daughters. She is the queen of all women in Paradise. According to Imām Subkī and Sirājuddīn Bulqīnī, Sayyidah Fāţimah is the superior-most among women, then comes her mother Sayyidah Khadījah and then Sayyidah Áayishah رضي الله عنهن. Since there are reports that suggest both possibilities – that Sayyidah Fāţimah is superior to Sayyidah Áayishah and vice-versa, it is better to remain silent on this issue. Sayyidah Fāţimah was married to our Master Álī رضي الله عنه, and she is the mother of Imām Ĥasan and Imām Ĥusayn رضي الله عنهم. She passed away five months after the departing of RasūlAllāh ﷺ at the age of twenty-five or twenty-nine.

[92] Yazīd is the son of Amīr Muáāwiyah رضي الله عنه. His army besieged Imām Ĥusayn's رضي الله عنه party and martyred most of them, including Imām Ĥusayn رضي الله عنه in Karbalā; the survivors were taken

41. The faith of a person by imitating[93] others is valid[94]
There are clear-cut proofs favouring this opinion.[95]

42. A sane person is not excused to cite ignorance as a reason
For not knowing the Creator of all things, small or great.[96]

---

to Syria and from there, were returned to Madīnah. Yazīd claimed that he had not ordered his army to kill the Imām, but only to arrest him and bring him to Damascus. Some scholars have cursed him, others have said that he should not be cursed, as we do not know for certain that he died as a disbeliever. In fact, it is not permissible to curse anyone by name, unless we have proof that such a person has indeed died without faith; this is not possible except by the informing of Allāh ﷻ, and being conveyed to us by the Prophet ﷺ. See the paper *Cursing Yazīd* [Ridawi Press] which is a compilation of citations from various works on this topic, refuting a speech-maker in the UK who slandered Imām Ghazālī by claiming that he was inimical to Ahl al-Bayt and that Imām Ghazālī was an admirer of Yazīd.

[93] *Taqlīd*: Accepting the opinion of another person without requiring evidence. According to the Mútazilah and some Ashárī scholars, the belief of a person is invalid upon merely accepting another person's word, and unless he has understood the proofs for beliefs he is not a believer. It is reported that Imām Abu'l Ĥasan al-Ashárī said that it is not sufficient that a person know about a creedal matter, and that he/she should know the basis and rational proofs for that issue. However, the faith of a person accepting belief by imitating others is valid according to all the four imāms, even though the person will be sinful for not learning the bases and proofs for one's beliefs. [Summarised from Qārī's commentary].

[94] The Prophet ﷺ, his companions and their followers accepted bedouins [*aárāb*] as believers without requiring them to investigate or to understand the sources from which principles of faith are derived. If it were indeed a requisite condition for faith, they would not have omitted it. [Shaykh Zādah, *Nażm al-Farayid*, #26].

[95] This is the opinion of the imāms Abū Ĥanīfah, Sufyān al-Thawrī, Mālik, Awzāýī, Shāfiýī, Aĥmad and most of the jurists رحمهم الله. They say, that the faith of a follower is valid, but he/she is sinful for not investigating and comprehending the proofs for his/her belief. Some of them have claimed consensus for this opinion. [Álī al-Qārī, *Minaĥ al-Rawđ*, p.216].

[96] If the message of Islām does not reach a person of sound mind, is it still obligatory for him to bear faith in Allāh ﷻ? If such a person does not believe in Allāh, does he go to Hell? If he does, will he stay there forever? Most of our Ĥanafī [i.e. Māturīdī] imāms said that a person of sound mind cannot cite ignorance for not believing in a Creator. Imām Abu'l

43. The belief of a person, in the throes of death[97] is not acceptable; for his lack of faith, prior.

44. Actions, good deeds are not counted as components – of Faith; though, there is a necessary affiliation.[98]

Ĥasan Ashárī and Abu'l Yusr al-Pazdawī [among Ĥanafīs] said that such a person has a valid excuse. The third opinion of some scholars is that though it is obligatory for such a person to have faith in a Creator, he will not be punished for not believing. Incidentally, all three opinions are reported from Imām Abū Ĥanīfah ﷺ. Bājūrī says in *Tuĥfah*, #12: It is therefore, that Abū Manşūr Māturīdī has said: "Our scholars have agreed that the commonfolk are believers and know their Lord, and are the filling of Paradise, as many reports indicate and there is consensus [*ijmāá*] on this; because they are naturally inclined to believe in the Unity of the Creator [*tawĥīd al-şāniý*], and that He is Pre-eternal and that everything else is created [*ĥādith*] even if they are unable to explain it in the manner of theologians [*mutakallimīn*] or describe it using their terminology".

[97] *Ba'as* means hardship or punishment; in another version the word used is *ya'as*, meaning when all hope is lost. In the Qur'ān: ***But their [accepting] faith did not benefit them, when they saw Our punishment***...[Ghāfir, 40:85]. It is said, that *ba'as* used in this verse means the throes of death, a while before the final gasps, when one beholds the angels of death, hitherto hidden from his eyes. In another Qur'ānic verse: ***And repentance is not [accepted] from those who keep sinning until death comes to them; and one of them says [at the time of death,] 'I repent now', or of those who die as disbelievers***...[Nisā'a, 4:18]. In a ĥadīth narrated by Ibn Úmar ﷺ, the Prophet ﷺ said: *Indeed, Allāh ﷻ will accept the repentance of His slave until the final gasp.* [Tirmidhī, #3537]. The final gasps [agonal respiration] before death [*ghargharah*] is a time of intense hardship [*ba'as*] and the moment of utter despair [*ya'as*].

[98] Imām Abū Ĥanīfah and most of his followers said: "Faith is affirmation of belief by the tongue; to accept it in the heart – even if a person does not do any good deed. A person who [sincerely] accepts all the tenets of Islām, remains a true believer even if he does not act upon any obligation or Islamic ruling." This is also the opinion of Mālik and Awzāýī. [Ibn Adhbah, *Rawđah al-Bahiyyah*, #7]. However, performing actions such as prayer, zakāt, fasting, pilgrimage etc. are obligations which bring one closer to faith, strengthen one's faith and are an outcome of faith; yet, they are not components of faith. [Qārī:] It is also the opinion of Imām al-Ĥaramayn and majority of Ashárīs; in *Sharĥ al-Maqāşid*, Taftāzānī has said that Ĥadīth scholars have favoured this opinion.

45. A person is not ruled a disbeliever or an apostate[99]
For sins such as adultery, murder or tyranny.[100]

46. Whoever considers becoming an apostate[101] in the future[102]
Is ejected and severed from religion[103] forthwith.

---

[99] The Khawārij say that a person becomes a kāfir, a disbeliever, by committing a sin – whether an enormity or a small sin [*kabīrah* or *ṣaghīrah*]. The Mútazilah say that such a person is neither a believer, nor a disbeliever – and they claim an intermediate state they call as 'transgression' and the person a transgressor [*fisq, fāsiq*]. We, the Ahl al-Sunnah say that regardless of the enormity of a person's sin, he remains a believer; and Allāh may punish him or forgive him.

[100] *Ikhtizāl*, means expropriation of another's property – whether by stealing, robbery or embezzlement. Here it is used as a generic term for the abuse of rights.

[101] ***Apostasy***: To sever the [bonds] of Islām, whether saying or doing something intentionally that is disbelief. Regardless of whether such a thing was said in derision, or in denial or actual belief [in such kufr]. [Thus] whosoever disbelieves in the Creator or Messengers or belies a Messenger or considers a ȟarām acknowledged by ijmāá, like adultery, as ȟalāl or vice-versa; or rejects that deemed obligatory by ijmāá or vice-versa; or intends to become a kāfir on the morrow or vacillates concerning the issue – in all such cases, the person becomes an apostate. [Among] actions that cause apostasy: any deliberate action which explicitly mocks religion, repudiation and disparagement of religion, such as casting a copy of the Qur'ān in garbage or prostrating to an idol or to the sun. However, children, the insane and those under duress are exempt from this ruling [if they utter words or commit deeds that cause apostasy]. Apostasy committed by an inebriated person is culpable, just as his Islām is valid; and the testimony concerning apostasy is absolutely admissible. [Imām Nawawī, *Minhāju't Ṭālibīn* p.501] **NOTE**: Apostasy in inebriation mentioned above is the Shāfiýī position; see distich #48 below for the Ȟanafī position.

[102] If a person contemplates apostasy – *al-íyādhu billāh* – and plans to renounce the religion of Islām sometime in the future, he/she will instantly become an apostate. RasūlAllāh ﷺ has said foretelling tribulations: "Hasten to do good deeds before strife and corruption [*fitnah*] come, like the parts of a dark night; [when] a man is a believer in the morning and becomes a kāfir in the evening, or a believer in the evening will become a kāfir by next morning. [Such] people will sell their religion for worldly benefit." [*Muslim* #118].

[103] The religion of Islām, which is the only path to salvation in the Hereafter.

47. Uttering a word of disbelief, even without believing in it
If said willingly,[104] is rejection of religion by heedlessness.[105]

48. One will not be ruled an apostate, when inebriated[106] –
He raves in his delirium and blabbers[107] disbelief.

---

[104] Knowingly, willingly and without compulsion; because, uttering kufr in duress or under coercion is excused as mentioned in the Qur'ān: ***Whoever disbelieves in Allāh after having believed in Him – except who is under compulsion while his heart is at peace concerning Islām; but the one who disbelieved with an open-heart, upon him is the Wrath of Allāh and for them [disbelievers] is a great punishment.*** [Nañl 16:106]. Poor Muslim farmers are being lynched in North India nowadays, by impotent thugs who call themselves 'cow protectors'. Muslims are forced to utter kufr such as 'Jai Shri Ram,' which is praise of their idols. If a Muslim says this to save his life or escape torture inflicted by merciless cowards [because dozens of bestial scoundrels surround lone helpless men], he will be excused. May Allāh táālā destroy the enemies of Muslims.

[105] If one utters kufr willingly he becomes a kāfir, even if he is convinced and unperturbed about Islām in his heart. In this case, Islām in his heart will not avail him. Movie actors, for example, do all kinds of antics and claim that Islām is in their hearts and they are only play-acting or saying something which they do not really believe in their hearts. Similarly, some people tell blasphemous jokes and when reproached, they justify their actions claiming that Islām is firm in their hearts. We seek Allāh's refuge. See *The Killer Mistake*, Riđawī Press for a lengthier discussion. When one becomes an apostate, all his good deeds are voided; his marriage is annulled. If he renews his faith and reverts to Islam, he will have to renew his marriage; furthermore, according to Ĥanafīs, if he had performed the obligatory pilgrimage earlier, he will be required to repeat it. We ask Allāh ﷻ to protect us from all kinds of disbelief.

[106] *Sukr* – inebriation. There are two cases of being stupefied:

1. Under the influence of drugs that cause a temporary lapse in consciousness, cause drowsiness or intoxication. Such as opium used in medicine [in the past] or any modern drug – pills, syrup etc. – for medicinal purposes. In such a case, anything a person does, including divorce is not valid.
2. Intoxication from prohibited substances such as alcohol and narcotics. In this case, divorce and other actions are considered valid, except for apostasy. One is not ruled an apostate for committing disbelief in a state of inebriation.

[107] Even actions – such as disrespecting a copy of the Qur'ān – can cause apostasy.

49. The 'Non-Existent'[108] cannot be seen;[109] nor is it a thing[110]
By evidence, resplendent like the munificent crescent.[111]

---

[108] *Mádūm* = non-existent. This is the opposite of *mawjūd* = something that exists. There are two kinds of *mádūm:* The first is *mádum basīṭ* [simply non-existent] one which is possible to exist, but does not exist. The second is *mádūm mumtaniý al-wujūd li-dhātih* [intrinsically impossible to exist], such as a hypothetical 'thing' where the opposites coincide or self-contradictory things. Falsehood in Divine Speech is also intrinsically impossible as it would negate Absolute Truth.

[109] Ibn Jamāáh [in *Daraj al-Máālī*]: There are two issues discussed in this distich.

1. Can Allāh ﷻ 'See' the non-existent or not? The Mútazilah say 'yes' and Ĥanafīs say 'no'.
2. Is the non-existent termed a 'thing' or an 'entity'? The Mútazilah say 'yes' and the Ahl al-Sunnah say 'no'.

[110] The Mútazilah say that *mádūm* is a 'thing', an 'entity' – *shayy* – and that all things are established even before their coming into existence, but are hidden, similar to clothes being concealed in a suitcase. The Ahl al-Sunnah say that the non-existent is NOT a thing, regardless of its being possible to exist or impossible to exist [Bājūrī in *Tuĥfah*, #122]. In the Qur'ān: ***And I created you, prior to which you were nothing*** [Maryam, 19:9]. In another verse: ***Indeed, there has passed a time upon the human, when he was not even a thing mentioned anywhere*** [Insān, 76:1]. Here the non-existent is described as 'not a thing' or 'nothing'. The latter verse means: 'a time has passed, when man was not a thing worth mention' and the word 'upon' is used due to the idiomatic expression.

The Mútazilah say, citing the Qur'ānic verse: ***Indeed, the tremor of the Final Hour is a terrible thing*** [Ĥajj, 22:1]. They say that the Hour has not occurred, nor the tremor; but it has been described as a 'thing' even though it has hitherto not come into existence.

This actually means that it WILL be a terrible thing when it occurs, not that it is a 'thing' right now. Moreover, Allāh táālā knows that it will certainly occur. According to research scholars, being a 'thing' is synonymous to being existent [*wujūd*] and not being a thing is synonymous to non-existence [*ádam*]. Sharīf Jurjānī has said that it has been linguistically accepted down the ages that 'thing' is used to refer to something that exists and 'No-thing' means non-existent [summarised from Qārī's commentary].

[111] That is, "by proofs and knowledge that is apparent to me like the munificent crescent". Also, the author hints that the crescent is named a 'shining crescent' only after the birth of the new moon and it can be seen; not when it is hidden and we are unable to see it. Similarly, only things that exist can be seen [*Jāmiý al-La'ālī*, p.130].

50. The two[112] are different: the created[113] is not a thing
Same as 'creating';[114] take it to illuminate your insight.[115]

---

[112] *Takwīn* = the ability to create, Creating Power; *mukawwan* = the thing that is created. *Takwīn* and *mukawwan* are two different things – they are not the same; one is the cause [*musabbib*] and the other is the effect [*musabbab*]. This is the belief of Ahl al-Sunnah; the Mútazilah believe that both are the same and both are accidents; i.e. came into existence later and are not pre-eternal [*qadīm*]. The Ashárīs say that *takwīn* is not a separate attribute but is actually a manifestation of Divine Power, which they term as the Effecting Power [*qudrah tanjīzīyyah*]; according to them, Divine Power is pre-eternal, but the Attributes of Action such as bringing to life, giving death, giving sustenance etc. are all accidents, and is the effect of exercising Divine Power.

[113] *Mukawwan.*

[114] *Takwīn.* To bring something into existense [*yījād*] from non-existence [*ádam*]. According to Ĥanafī imāms, *takwīn* is the eighth Divine Attribute [*ṣifah dhātīyah*], which is in addition to Divine Power and Divine Will [*qudrah, irādah*] and distinct from both. This, like all other Attributes, is also beginningless, pre-eternal, interminable, unendingly eternal and self-subsisting.

[115] Kohl is believed to illuminate the eyes; here, the couplet means: remember that *takwīn* and *mukawwan* are separate; take this opinion to illuminate your insight [Qārī].

Musāyarah/Musāmarah: This issue revolves around the Attributes of Action [*ṣifāt al-afáāl*], the existence of which is known by verses such as: ***The Creator, the Maker, the Originator of forms*** [Ĥashr 59:24]. Similar are the names, Giver of Sustenance, Giver of Life and Giver of Death [*rāziq, muĥyī, mumīt*]. These are attributes that imply an effect; and they have names other than Divine Power [*qudrah*], and are named according to the effect that is produced – and all these attributes are grouped under one name: *takwīn;* that is, all the Attributes of Action are grouped under one term. Thus, if the effect produced is creation, then the Divine Name [on account of this action] is Creator [*khāliq*] and the Attribute is Creating [*khalq*]. If the effect is sustenance [*rizq*], the Name is Giver of Sustenance [*rāziq/razzāq*], and the Attribute is Giving Sustenance [*tarzīq*]; if the effect is life [*ĥayāh*], the Name that implies the attribute is Giver of Life [*muĥyī*] and the attribute is Giving of Life [*iĥyā'a*]; if the effect is death [*mawt*], the Name that indicates the attribute is Giver of Death [*mumīt*] and the attribute is Giving of Death [imātah]. But all these Attributes of Action converge under one attribute, and that is *takwīn*.

Musayarah/Musāmarah [summarised]: The Asháris say: *Takwīn* is not a distinct or a separate attribute, and no more than Divine Power, when it is linked to a specific action. Thus, To Create [*takhlīq*] is Divine Power related to bringing creation into existence; Giving Sustenance [*tarzīq*] is Divine Power related to providing sustenance – and since Attributes of Action are actually 'relation of' Divine Power to something that occurs, they are accidents [*ĥādith*].

Bājūrī in *Tuĥfah* #30: They differed concerning *takwīn*; The Māturīdīs affirmed *takwīn* as a Divine Attribute which is beginningless, pre-eternal and subsisting by Allāh Himself – and it is by this Attribute He brings into existence or annihilates something. But if it is related to existence, it is known as 'Bringing into Existence' [*yījād*], if it is related to annihilation, it is known as 'Annihilation' [*iýdām*]; if it is related to life, it is known as 'Giving Life' [*iĥyā'a*], etc. Thus, according to Māturīdīs, the Attributes of Action [*șifāt al-afáāl*] are beginningless and pre-eternal because they are [all actually under one term:] the Attribute of Creating [*takwīn*] – some have said that they are all separate attributes, which is debated by ancient scholars. Asháris do not accept this and say that Attributes of Action are relation of Divine Power in Execution [*tanjīzīyyah*], which are accidents.

Abū Ádhabah in *Rawđah al-Bahiyyah*: Ibn al-Ghars al-Ĥanafī [833-894AH] has said: *Takwīn* is a term used to describe the act of creation, of bringing into existence and other Divine Actions. This is an Attribute of His Self and it subsists by Allāh Himself. That is to say, Allāh has brought into existence every particle in this universe, and everything comes into existence at the time He has ordained – and the exact time of its coming into existence is known to Allāh ﷻ and is linked to His Will. *Takwīn* is pre-eternal, similar to Divine Will; but its connection to the creation is an accident. But one cannot say that the Power to Create [*takwīn*] does not exist until the creation [*mukawwan*] exists, just as 'hitting' does not exist unless the object that can be hit exists, unlike knowledge or power [i.e. the action requiring an object, such as hitting a thing, cannot exist until the object exists; unlike knowledge or power concerning that object which can exist prior to the existence of the object]; because we [Māturīdīs] say that *takwīn* has two meanings:

1. The Attribute of Self [*șifat nafsiyyah*] which is the intrinsic ability to create and bring into existence [every contingent thing].

2. The Divine Act of creation: this is the relation of the Attribute of Self to the thing that is created [at the time of its creation].

That which the Māturīdīs profess to be pre-eternal is the Attribute, not the Action per se.

[Abū Ádhabah continues:] Know that the Ĥanafis derive the concept of *takwīn* from the Qur'ān, where Allāh ﷻ says: ***Indeed, Our saying to a thing, when We Will for it [to exist], that We say 'Be' and it becomes*** [Naĥl, 16:40]. So they say, the word 'Be' [*kun*] precedes the existince of that thing, and this is known as the 'Command' [*amr*] and the 'Word'. [Māturīdīs say:] Allāh ﷻ has described *takwīn* by the word, 'Be' [*kun*] and the created thing [*mukawwan*] by the word, 'so it becomes' [*fa-yakūn*]. The words *takwīn, ikhtirāá* [to originate], *yījād* [to bring into existence], *khalq* [to create] are all synonymous in one aspect and are dissimilar in another. They mean the same in the sense 'a thing that is brought into existence, and previously it was non-existent' and this [attribute] has a more specific relation than Divine Power [*qudrah*] to that thing. Because Divine Power has the same relation concerning all things subject to Divine Power [*maqdūrāt*]; but *takwīn* is related only to those things [*maqdūrāt*] which can come into existence; and this is not [merely] a relative attribute [*ṣifah nisbiyyah*] that can only be understood in the context of something to which it is related – rather, it is a [definitive] attribute that is evinced by the result that is produced by that relation [i.e. Giving Life is manifested by life]. As for the claim that [Māturīdīs] say 'Divine Power is effective in the possibility of a thing', such an ascription to them is incorrect. Rather, according to them, Divine Power is related to a thing [*maqdūr*] concerning its possibility to exist; and *takwīn* is related to bringing that thing into existence and is the cause that brings it into existence; its relation to the action-accident [*fiýl ĥādith*] is similar to Divine Will concerning something that is willed [*murād*]. However, everything that is subject to Divine Power and everything that is in Divine Knowledge need not necessarily exist; only *takwīn* brings a thing into existence. Therefore this attribute is pre-eternal, because accidents cannot subsist in the Self of Allāh ﷻ.

Shaykh-Zādah Ábd al-Raĥīm in his *Nażm al-Farāyid* #10: Ashárīs say that *takwīn* is not a separate attribute of Allāh ﷻ; rather it is a nominal description, an abstract concept, that is the relation of the cause with its effect as mentioned in *Sharĥ Jawharah, Musāyarah, Maqāṣid*, etc. Ĥanafī scholars say that it is agreed by consensus, and the evidence for which is found in revelation and reason both, that Allāh ﷻ has brought the creation into existence and has created this universe; and to affirm a name derived from the word denoting an attribute, without that attribute being present, is an absolute impossibility – else it would imply the presence of an effect without the attribute that brought about that effect [i.e., since Allāh ﷻ has been named the Creator, Originator, He must have the attributes of being able to create and to originate, *takhlīq*].

It is mentioned in the Book of Allāh ﷻ that ***He has Power over all things*** [Baqarah, 2:20] and also ***He is the Creator of every thing*** [Anáām, 6:101/102]. Now, 'all things possible' [*maqdūrāt*] were not present in pre-eternity, just as creation [*makhlūqāt*] did not exist –

so to affirm one attribute [*qudrah*] in pre-eternity and deny another [*takwīn*], by bringing the latter under the rubric of the former and attempt to redefine the meanings of both; this is nothing but high-handedness.

The Ashárīs say that, if the meaning of *takwīn* is 'the very influence that Power exercises in a thing that is subject to it', then it is a relative attribute. It is not present unless the thing to which it is related [*muntasib*] is present, then the accidence of a created thing [*ĥudūth al-mukawwan*] necessitates the accidence of the Creating Power [*takwīn*]. But if it is taken to mean the effecting attribute [the cause] in the existence of the effect, then it is Divine Power itself...

[Answering the above objection, Shaykh-Zadah says:] Indeed, the Attribute of Allāh ﷻ in bringing about the existence of the creation is *takwīn*, and it is a causal attribute influencing the existence of the effect. Divine Power is another attribute of Allāh ﷻ, which means that the influence CAN be exercised.

Takwīn is more specific than Power [*qudrah*]; because *qudrah* has equal relation concerning all things that are subject to it [*maqdūrāt*]; and *takwīn* is related only to those that have/will come into existence. Qudrah does not necessitate that everything subject to it will exist; but *takwīn* entails that the thing to which it is related, will come into existence...

Ţaĥāwī in his *Áqīdah*: And just as Allāh ﷻ is Pre-eternal, beginningless with all His Attributes, so also is He, and His Attributes eternal, unending, interminable [*azalī, abadī*]. It is not that He gained the name 'Creator' only after He made the creation; nor did He come to be known as the Originator [*bāriy*] only after the origination of the universe – rather, He was the Sustainer [*rabb*] when none existed whom He sustains [*marbūb*]; He was very much the Creator, even when there was no creation. Just as He is entitled to the name 'He who Resurrects the dead' [*muĥyi'l mawtā*] even before resurrecting them, He is entitled to be called the 'Creator' before He created the universe – and that is because He has Power over all things.

Allāh ﷻ knows best.

51. Unlawful food is also sustenance, similar to lawful food[116]
Even if our adversaries dislike my saying it thus.

52. In the graves,[117] about the One-ness [*tawĥīd*] of Allāh,
Every person after death, will be questioned.[118]

---

[116] The Mútazilah claim that unlawful food or wealth and property gained by illegitimate means are not deemed sustenance [*rizq*] because, according to them, Allāh ﷻ does not give unlawful sustenance [*rizq ĥarām*]. The Ahl al-Sunnah say that everything that one gets, is sustenance given by Allāh, whether one acquires it by lawful or unlawful means. The reason for this contention is the definition of *rizq* – the Ahl al-Sunnah define it as anything that nourishes the body of a living being; the Mútazilah say that *rizq* means rightful ownership, which obviously, is an invalid definition [Bakrī].

[117] Even though, only the grave is mentioned, every soul will be questioned wherever it is confined after death – whether a person had drowned or was burned or eaten by a wild animal or embalmed, or eaten by scavenger birds, as it happens in the *Sky Burial* in Tibet or the isolation of dead bodies in the *Tower of Silence* by the Zoroastrians.

[118] Two fierce angels, *Munkar* and *Nakīr,* will interrogate a person after his/her death, in a terrible manner asking these three questions: 1) Who is your Lord? 2) What is your Religion? 3) What did you say about this Person? [referring to our Master Muĥammad ﷺ]. Believers [Muslims] will reply: "My Lord is Allāh; my Religion is Islām; and my Prophet is Sayyidunā Muĥammad ﷺ." The disbelievers/kāfir and hypocrites/munāfiq will say: "Alas! Alas! I do not know."

In the ĥadīth reported by Qatādah from Anas ibn Mālik : When a slave [i.e. a person] is placed in his grave, and his companions [friends and relatives] turn back and he [the dead man] hears their footsteps fade away, two angels will come to him, will make him sit up and tell him: 'What did you say about this man' pointing towards Muĥammad ﷺ. The believer will reply: 'I bear witness that he is the slave of Allāh and His Messenger.' The person will be told: 'Look at this [potential] seat of yours in hell, but Allāh ﷻ has replaced it with a place for you in paradise.' The believer will see both the places.' [*Bukhārī*, #1374].

There are reports that some people will be exempt from questioning, such as martyrs, Muslim soldiers guarding the outposts of Muslim lands, those who die on Fridays (whether in the day or in the night), those who recite Sūrah al-Mulk every night, and those who die of internal diseases [in the ĥadīth, cholera is mentioned, *mabţūn*].

53. Disbelievers and sinners will be meted out[119]
punishment in the grave – recompense for evil deeds.[120]

54. People will enter Paradise only by the Grace[121]
Of Raĥmān. Know this O people with high hopes.[122]

---

[119] Disbelievers will be punished in the grave; and some sinful Muslims will also be punished in the grave. This line is rendered varyingly in different versions of the text; ***yuqđā***, meaning 'will be subject to' or ***bughdā***, 'those who despised and bore animosity to God' or ***ba'ađun***, meaning, some of the sinners will be punished.

[120] In the ĥadīth: *Punishment in the grave is real and true* [*Bukhārī*, #1372]. The following prayer was taught by RasūlAllāh ﷺ to seek refuge of Allāh from the torment in the grave: ***allāhumma innī a'úūdhu bika min fitnati'n nār wa min ádhābi'n nār; wa a'úūdhu bika min fitnati'l qabr; wa a'úūdhu bika min fitnati'l ghinā, wa a'úūdhu bika min fitnati'l faqr; wa a'úūdhu bika min fitnati'l masīĥ al-dajjāl*** – O Allāh, I seek Your refuge from the ordeal of fire and the torment of fire and the severe test in the grave; I seek Your refuge from the seduction of wealth, and I seek Your refuge from the misery of poverty; and I seek Your refuge from the turmoil of Dajjāl, the false messiah [*Bukhārī*, #6376].

In another ĥadīth, RasūlAllāh ﷺ is reported to have said: *The grave is either a garden from the gardens of paradise, or a pit of fire from hell* [*Tirmidhī*, #2460].

[121] Believers will not enter paradise just on account of their good deeds. Rather, it will be due to the Grace of Allāh ﷻ and His Conferring honour upon His slaves. This is mentioned in the ĥadīth where RasūlAllāh ﷺ said: *None of you will enter paradise because of his deeds. His companions asked: "Not even you, O Messenger of Allāh?" He replied: "Not even I; except that Allāh ﷻ has enveloped me in His Mercy"* [*Bukhārī*, #5673]. The Jahmiyyah, Qadariyyah, Najjāriyyah and Mútazilah rejected this, and said that it is obligatory upon Allāh ﷻ to grant paradise for those who do good deeds. The Ahl al-Sunnah say that nothing is obligatory upon Allāh ﷻ.

Yet, this does not contradict the Quranic verse: ***Enter paradise for the [good] deeds you used to do*** [Naĥl, 16:32] as people will be in different levels of paradise, according to their deeds.

[122] Those who hope to be forgiven and enter paradise.

55. The Reckoning[123] after the Resurrection[124] is true
Be wary of committing sins [for they will be accounted].[125]

56. Some will be given their deed-books[126] in their right hands[127]
Some behind their backs,[128] and some in their left hands.[129]

---

[123] People will be accounted for their deeds; this is known as *ĥisāb*, or the Reckoning. The Jahmiyyah and philosophers reject the concept of Reckoning.

[124] The Accounting of Deeds will happen after people are brought forth from their graves. When it is such a grave matter, people should be wary of transgressing the Rights of Allāh and especially be cautious from violating the rights of humans. However, this refers to sins in general, and they are indeed a heavy burden. *Astaghfirullāh.*

[125] It is an article of faith to believe in life after death and in the Day of Resurrection and the Great Gathering [*yawm al-ĥashr wa'n nushūr*] as Allāh ﷻ has mentioned in the Qur'ān: ***Soon his account shall be taken, and [he will be] accounted in an easy manner*** [Inshiqāq, 84:8]. In another verse: ***Read [aloud] your record; you suffice [for yourself] on this day to take the account of your own self*** [Isrā'a, 17:14].

[126] The *ĥafażah* or the guardian angels; also known as *kirāman kātibīn*, the 'honourable scribes', record our deeds – it is reported that every one of us has four recording angels; two in the daytime and two in the night. [See Suyūṭī's *Ĥabāyik*, p.89, #314].

[127] Muslims will be given their records of deeds in their right hands. At the time of examination, some will be examined very swiftly and lightly; his good deeds will be rewarded and his sins will be forgiven. Anyone who is questioned, will face dire consequences. We seek Allāh's refuge from being questioned, and to be included among those who are totally exempt and sent into paradise without any accounting. Āmīn.

[128] Disbelievers and hypocrites will be given their record of deeds in their left hands or worse, in their left hands twisted behind their backs.

[129] This is mentioned in the Qur'ān: ***As for him, whose book of deeds is given in his right hand; soon his account shall be taken, and [he shall be] accounted in an easy manner; and he shall return to his family in happiness; as for him, whose book of deeds is given behind his back; soon he shall cry out for extermination; [but] he will be sent into a blazing fire*** [Inshiqāq, 84:7-12]. In another verse: ***As for him, who is given his book of deeds in his left hand, he will say 'Alas! Were it that my book of deeds had never been given to me and were it that I knew nothing of my account'*** [Ĥāqqah, 69:25-26].

57. Weighing of Deeds[130] is true, and so is the Crossing –
Upon the Bridge,[131] without any doubt.

---

[130] Allāh ﷻ has said: ***And the Weighing [of deeds] on that day is true. They, whose scales are heavy are indeed the successful ones. And they, whose scales are meagre are the ones who have put their own selves into peril and a loss – recompense for their unjust rejection of Our signs*** [Aáráf, 7:8-9]. In another verse: ***And We shall place the Scales of Justice on the Day of Resurrection..*** [Anbiyā'a, 21:47].

Qārī: Deeds or actions are abstract, intangible – one cannot imagine their essences or their being heavy or light; nor can one visualise their being weighed from a physical perspective. But as it has been mentioned in the Qur'ān, and we must believe, without trying to investigate the nature of these things – because Allāh ﷻ has the Power to make His slaves understand or measure their deeds. Many exegetes have said that it is a physical scale with pans [for placing deeds] and with a pointer.

[131] *Ṣirāt* is a long bridge on the brim of hell, passing through its middle; the bridge is finer than hair, sharper than the blade of a sword and darker than the night – everyone has to pass on this bridge. There will be grappling irons and sharp hooks [*kalālīb*] suspended on either side of the bridge. Those who cross the bridge, will enter paradise and those who slip will fall into hell. It is mentioned in the Qur'ān: ***And there is none among you, except that he will have to cross [the bridge] upon hell*** [Maryam, 19:71]. Qarāfī, Shaykh Ibn Ábd al-Salām, Zarkashī and others have said that the description 'finer than hair, sharper than sword', is figurative if the description is indeed established by authentic narrations. Bayhaqī has said: 'I did not find this description in any authentic narration; however, it has been described thus, by companions, and in their own words.' This has also been explained thus: It is a very delicate and serious matter – hence, finer than hair; and a grave and perilious journey – hence, sharper than a sword. Allāh ﷻ knows best [Summarised from Laqqāni's commentary *Hadiyyatu'l Murīd* 2/1097, #106].

Muslims will swiftly cross the bridge. Some will pass on it in the blink of an eye, some with the speed of lightning, some as a swift breeze, some as galloping horses and some as though riding a camel. Some will cross the bridge in safety, some will be bruised and battered but will eventually cross the bridge, and some others will fall from the bridge into hell. The last ones to pass will be dragging themselves, and will be pulled towards safety. [Relevant portion summarised from a lengthy ĥadīth in *Bukhārī*, #6573]. In another ĥadīth, RasūlAllāh ﷺ said: And your Prophet will be upon the bridge praying for you, beseeching: 'O my Allāh, let them pass in safety. Let them be safe, *rabbi sallim, sallim* [*Muslim*, #195].

58. It is hoped that the righteous ones will intercede[132]
For sinners with huge sins, big as mountains.[133]

59. Prayers have a definite benefit[134]and a profound effect[135]
It is the heretics who reject; and claim prayers are futile.[136]

---

[132] Pious people, righteous folk such as Prophets, Awliyā'a, martyrs, upright scholars and pious Muslims will intercede for those who have committed sins – whether major or minor. Ibn Jamāáh has said, 'All people can be classified into two categories: Believers and disbelievers. Everyone concurs that disbelievers will be in hell [there is no dispute that the *kāfir* will be in hell]. Believers are of two kinds: the pious ones and the sinners. It is agreed by consensus, that righteous Muslims will be in paradise. Sinners who are believers will be of two kinds: sinners who have repented and sinners who have not repented. It is agreed by consensus that the sinner who has repented will be in paradise. That leaves the sinner who has not repented, and his fate will be decided by the Mercy of Allāh ﷻ.

Be it known, that our Prophet, our Master Muĥammad ﷺ is the chief of all intercessors. He will be the first to intercede, and his intercession will be the first to be accepted. Many ĥadīth mention the exalted station granted to our Master ﷺ on that day. In the Qur'ān: ***Nigh it is, that your Lord Sustainer will bring you forth upon the Extolled Station*** [Isrā'a, 17:79]. Exegetes have said that *maqāman maĥmūdā* refers to the high station given to RasūlAllāh ﷺ on Judgement Day, when he will be extolled; others have said that it may also mean the high station of intercession.

[133] All sins except idolatry and polytheism [*shirk*] may be forgiven, as Allāh ﷻ has Himself said: ***Indeed, Allāh will not forgive that partners be ascribed to him [or commiting kufr]; but may forgive anything besides, for whomsoever He Wills.*** [Nisā'a, 4:48].

[134] Prayers [*duáā*], beseeching Allāh ﷻ and asking Him for favours, forgiveness, protection from adversity and for warding off danger, prolonging one's life, asking for children, etc., are all permissible; and prayers will be answered. Allāh ﷻ has said: ***Call upon Me; I will Answer your (prayers)*** [Ghāfir, 40:60]. RasūlAllāh ﷺ is reported to have said: *That which has been ordained will not be superseded, except by prayer* [Ĥākim in Mustadrak, #1814].

[135] Similarly the prayers of the living will benefit the dead, for their forgiveness, comfort in their graves and for elevation of their ranks.

[136] The Mútazilah say that prayers [duáā] are to no avail – because, according to them, all things are destined and prayers cannot change anything. They also deny that prayers of the living can benefit the dead.

60. This world of ours, the universe, is an accident[137] and Hyle[138]
Does not actually exist;[139] listen to this with delight.[140]

61. Paradise and Hell have already been created[141]
A time has already passed upon them so far.[142]

62. A person of faith will not stay forever
For the wretchedness of his sin, in the Abode of Flames.[143]

---

[137] *Ĥādith* - Accident: that which came into existence after having been non-existent. Ancient philosophers believed that the world, the universe, has existed eternally; but we Muslims believe that it was non-existent and it was brought into existence by the Creator.

[138] *Hayūlā*: Hyle, or Prime Matter according to Aristotle's theory of matter, which can be stated as: everything is made of four fundamental elements: earth, air, fire and water; these elements can be hot or cold, wet or dry. The concept of 'prime matter' is attributed to Aristotle, meaning it is the matter of the elements; and the elements are actually composed of this 'prime matter' [hyle] and the form that it takes - and that it can potentially, take any form. [See Ainsworth, Thomas: Form vs. Matter, Stanford Encyclopedia of Philosophy]

[139] According to philosophers, this hypothetical 'Prime Matter' is supposed to have existed eternally and is primordial; it exists without measure [*kammiyyah*] or attribute [*kayfiyyah*]; and it is not accompanied by an accident; and then it itself undertook attributes, and accidents occurred, and the world was created. Thus it is explained in *Qāmūs* [Qārī].

[140] We Muslims believe that everything was created by Allāh ﷻ, the Creator. Only He has existed pre-eternally, without a beginning. Everything is Created by His Will, subject to His Power, and His Creating [*takwīn*].

[141] Both Paradise and Hell have been created and a period of time has passed upon them, as mentioned in the Qur'ān: [*Paradise is already*] ***prepared for the pious*** [Aāl Ímrān, 3:133] and [*Hell is already*] ***prepared for the disbelievers*** [Baqarah, 2:24]. The two abodes exist and wil be everlasting as mentioned in the Qur'ān: ***They shall abide in it forever*** [Nisā'a, 4:57].

[142] Some Mútazilīs say that while Paradise and Hell are indeed true, they do not exist now and will be created in the Hereafter.

[143] According to the Ahl al-Sunnah, a person who commits the deadly sins [*kabīrah*] and dies without repentance, will not remain in Hell forever. The Khawārij and Mútazilah say that committing an enormity causes one to go out of faith.

63. I have fashioned a poem on *Tawĥīd*, the Correct Creed;
Beautiful in form; indeed, like sheer magic.

64. Giving solace to the heart and glad tidings of comfort
Reviving the soul, as pure water[144] [revitalises the body].

65. Engage with it, and memorise it; believe[145] in this creed[146]
You will attain immense blessings [in both worlds].

66. And help this poor slave evermore
By remembering him in your prayers.[147]

67. He fervently hopes that Allāh will forgive him, by His Grace
And will grant him eternal bliss in the Hereafter.

68. And I too shall pray as much as I can
For those who pray for me and wish me well.[148]

---

[144] Similar to pure and sweet water that invigorates the body of a thirsty man, this poem on the correct creed of Ahl al-Sunnah rejuvenates one's faith and revitalises the soul.

[145] The articles of faith mentioned in this poem are the true creed of Ahl al-Sunnah; the author exhorts Muslims to read it, memorise it and understand it well.

[146] This book covers almost all the necessary aspects of the Sunni Creed. Readers are encouraged to read *Áqīdah Ţaĥāwīyyah* which has some more topics not mentioned here.

[147] Pray for him, ask Allāh to forgive him [*istighfār*] whenever you remember him. We ask Allāh ﷻ to give Imām Álī al-Ūshī ؒ a great reward, and to elevate his rank in paradise.

[148] We ask Allāh ﷻ to have mercy upon the author, and all our teachers and shaykhs; our parents and our elders – we ask Allāh ﷻ to grant us and our friends and relatives, a beautiful ending and death upon faith; and grant us exalted stations in the hereafter in the company of Prophets, *siddīq*, martyrs and righteous folk. Praise belongs to Allāh ﷻ.

Appendix A

THE QAŞĪDAH IN ARABIC

1	yaqūlu'l ábdu fī bad-i'l amālī li tawĥīd^{in} bi nażm^{in} ka'l la-ālī	يَقُوْلُ الْـعَبْدُ فِي بَدْءِ الْأَمَالِي لِتَوْحِيْدٍ بِنَظْمٍ كَالَّلآلِي
2	ilāhu'l khalqi mawlānā qadīm^{un} wa mawşūf^{un} bi awşāfi'l kamāli	إِلٰهُ الْخَلْقِ مَوْلَانَا قَدِيْمٌ وَمَوْصُوْفٌ بِأَوْصَافِ الْكَمَالِ
3	huwa'l ĥayyu'l mudabbiru kulla amr^{in} huwa'l ĥaqqu'l muqaddiru dhu'l jalāli	هُوَ الْحَيُّ الْمُدَبِّرُ كُلَّ أَمْرٍ هُوَ الْحَقُّ الْمُقَدِّرُ ذُو الْجَلَالِ
4	murīdu'l khayri wa'sh sharri'l qabīĥi wa lākin laysa yarđā bi'l muĥāli	مُرِيْدُ الْخَيْرِ وَالشَّرِّ الْقَبِيْحِ وَلٰكِنْ لَيْسَ يَرْضَى بِالْمُحَالِ
5	şifātu'llāhi laysat áyna dhāt^{in} wa lā ghayra^{n} siwāhu dha^{n}fişāli	صِفَاتُ اللهِ لَيْسَتْ عَيْنَ ذَاتٍ وَلَا غَيْراً سِوَاهُ ذَا انْفِصَالِ
6	şifātu'dh dhāti wa'l afáāli ţurra^{n} qadīmāt^{un} maşūnātu'z zawālī	صِفَاتُ الذَّاتِ وَالْأَفْعَالِ طُرًّا قَدِيْمَاتٌ مَصُوْنَاتُ الزَّوَالِ
7	nusammi'llāha shayy'a^{n} lā ka'l ashyā'a wa dhāta^{n} án jihāti's sitti khālī	نُسَمِّي اللهَ شَيْئاً لَا كَالْأَشْيَاءِ وَذَاتاً عَنْ جِهَاتِ السِّتِّ خَالِي

8	wa laysa'l ismu ghayra^{n} li'l musammā ladā ahli'l başīrati khayri aāli	وَلَيْسَ الْاِسْمُ غَيراً لِلْـــمُسَمَّى لَــدَى أَهلِ الْــبَصِيْرَةِ خَيرِ آلِ
9	wa mā in jawhar^{un} rabbī wa jism^{un} wa lā kull^{un} wa baáđ^{un} dhu'shtimāli	وَمَـا إِنْ جَـوهَرٌ رَبِّي وَجِسْمٌ وَلَا كُلٌّ وَبَعْضٌ ذُو اشْـتِمَـالِ
10	wa fi'l adh-hāni ĥaqq^{un} kawnu juz'y^{in} bilā waşfi't tajazzī ya'bna khālī	وَفِي الْأَذْهَـانِ حَقٌّ كَوْنُ جُزْءٍ بِلَا وَصْفِ التَّجَزِّي يَا ابْنَ خَالِي
11	wa ma'l qur'ānu makhlūqa^{n} táālā kalāmu'r rabbi án jinsi'l maqāli	وَمَـا الْــقُرآنُ مَخْـلُوْقاً تَعَـالَى كَلَامُ الرَّبِّ عَنْ جِنْسِ الْمَقَالِ
12	wa rabbu'l árshi fawqa'l árshi lākin bilā waşfi't tamakkuni wa'ttişāli	وَرَبُّ الْعَرْشِ فَوْقَ الْعَرْشِ لٰكِنْ بِلَا وَصْفِ الــتَّمَــكُّنِ وَاتِّصَالِ
13	wa ma't tashbīhu li'r Raĥmāni waj'ha^{n} fa şun án dhāka aşnāfa'l ahālī	وَمَـا التَّشْبِيهُ لِلرَّحْمٰنِ وَجْــهاً فَصُنْ عَنْ ذَاكَ أَصْنَافَ الْأَهَالِي
14	wa lā yamđī ála'd dayyāni waqt^{un} wa azmān^{un} wa aĥwāl^{un} bi ĥāli	وَلَا يَـمْضِي عَلَى الــدَّيَّانِ وَقْتٌ وَأَزْمَـانٌ وَأَحْــوَالٌ بِحَــالِ
15	wa mustaghn^{in} ilāhī án nisā^{yin} wa awlād^{in} ināth^{in} aw rijāli	وَمُـسْتَغْنٍ إِلٰهِي عَـنْ نِسَــاءٍ وَأَوْلَادٍ إِنَـاثٍ أَوْ رِجَــالِ

16	kadhā án kulli dhī áwn^{in} wa naşr^{in} tafarrada dhu'l jalāli wa dhu'l máālī	كَذَا عَنْ كُلِّ ذِي عَوْنٍ وَنَصْرٍ تَفَرَّدَ ذُو الْجَلَالِ وَذُو الْمَعَالِي
17	yumītu'l khalqa qahra^{n} thumma yuĥyī fa yajzīhim álā wafqi'l khişāli	يُمِيتُ الْخَلْقَ قَهراً ثُمَّ يُحْيِي فَيَجْزِيهِمْ عَلَى وَفْقِ الْخِصَالِ
18	li ahli'l khayri jannāt^{un} wa númā wa li'l kuffāri idrāku'n nakāli	لِأَهْلِ الْخَيْرِ جَنَّاتٌ وَنُعْمَى وَلِلْكُفَّارِ إِدْرَاكُ النَّكَالِ
19	wa lā yafna'l jaĥīmu wa lā'l-jinānu wa lā ahlūhumā ahlu'ntiqāli	وَلَا يَفْنَى الْجَحِيمُ وَلَا الْجِنَانُ وَلَا أَهْلُوهُمَا أَهْلُ انْتِقَالِ
20	yarāhu'l mu-minūna bighayri kayf^{in} wa idrāk^{in} wa đarb^{in} min mithāli	يَرَاهُ الْمُؤْمِنُونَ بِغَيْرِ كَيْفٍ وَإِدْرَاكٍ وَضَرْبٍ مِنْ مِثَالِ
21	fa yansawna'n naýīma idhā ra-awhu fa yā khusrāna ahli'l iýtizāli	فَيَنْسَوْنَ النَّعِيمَ إِذَا رَأَوْهُ فَيَا خُسْرَانَ أَهْلِ الْإِعْتِزَالِ
22	wa mā in fiýlu^{n} aşlaĥa dha'ftirāđ^{in} ála'l hādi'l muqaddasi dhi't táālī	وَمَا إِنْ فِعْلُ أَصْلَحَ ذَا افْتِرَاضٍ عَلَى الْهَادِي الْمُقَدَّسِ ذِي التَّعَالِي
23	wa farđ^{un} lāzim^{un} taşdīqu rusl^{in} wa amlāk^{in} kirām^{in} bi'n nawāli	وَفَرْضٌ لَازِمٌ تَصْدِيقُ رُسْلٍ وَأَمْلَاكٍ كِرَامٍ بِالنَّوَالِ

24	wa khatmu'r rusli bi'ş şadri'l muállā nabiyy^{in} hāshimiyy^{in} dhī jamāli	وَخَتْمُ الرُّسْلِ بِالصَّدْرِ الْمُعَلَّى نَبِيٌّ هَاشِمِيٌّ ذِي جَمَالِ
25	imāmu'l anbiyā'yi bila'khtilāf^{in} wa tāju'l aşfiyāyi bila'khtilāli	إِمَامُ الْأَنْبِيَاءِ بِلَا اخْتِلَافٍ وَتَاجُ الْأَصْفِيَاءِ بِلَا اخْتِلَالِ
26	wa bāq^{in} sharúhu fī kulli waqt^{in} ilā yawmi'l qiyāmati wa'rtiĥāli	وَبَاقٍ شَرْعُهُ فِي كُلِّ وَقْتٍ إِلَىٰ يَوْمِ الْقِيَامَةِ وَارْتِحَالِ
27	wa ĥaqq^{un} amru miýrāj^{in} wa şidq^{un} fa fīhi naşşu akhbār^{in} áwālī	وَحَقٌّ أَمْرُ مِعْرَاجٍ وَصِدْقٌ فَفِيهِ نَصُّ أَخْبَارٍ عَوَالِي
28	wa marjuww^{un} shafāátu ahli khayr^{in} li aş-ĥābi'l kabāyiri ka'l jibāli	وَمَرْجُوٌّ شَفَاعَةُ أَهْلِ خَيْرٍ لِأَصْحَابِ الْكَبَائِرِ كَالْجِبَالِ
29	wa inna'l anbiyā-a lafī amān^{in} áni'l işyāni ámda^{n} wa'nýizāli	وَإِنَّ الْأَنْبِيَاءَ لَفِي أَمَانٍ عَنِ الْعِصْيَانِ عَمْداً وَانْعِزَالِ
30	wa mā kānat nabiyya^{n} qaţţu unthā wa lā ábd^{un} wa shakş^{un} dhu'ftiáāli	وَمَا كَانَتْ نَبِيّاً قَطُّ أُنْثَىٰ وَلَا عَبْدٌ وَشَخْصٌ ذُو افْتِعَالِ
31	wa dhu'l qarnayni lam yúraf nabiyya^{n} kadhā luqmānu faĥdhar án jidāli	وَذُو الْقَرْنَيْنِ لَمْ يُعْرَفْ نَبِيّاً كَذَا لُقْمَانُ فَاحْذَرْ عَنْ جِدَالِ

32	wa ýīsā sawfa ya'tī thumma yatwī li dajjāl^{in} shaqiyy^{in} dhī khabāli	وَعِيسَى سَوْفَ يَأْتِي ثُمَّ يَتْوِي لِدَجَّالٍ شَقِيٍّ ذِي خَبَالِ
33	karāmātu'l waliyyi bi dāri dunyā lahā kawn^{un} fahum ahlu'n nawāli	كَرَامَاتُ الْوَلِيِّ بِدَارِ دُنْيَا لَهَا كَوْنٌ فَهُمْ أَهْلُ النَّوَالِ
34	wa lam yafđu'l waliyy^{un} qaţţu dahra^{n} nabiyya^{n} aw rasūla^{n} fi'ntiĥāli	وَلَمْ يَفْضُلْ وَلِيٌّ قَطُّ دَهْرًا نَبِيًّا أَوْ رَسُولاً فِي انْتِحَالِ
35	wa li'ş şiddāqi rujĥān^{un} jaliyy^{un} ála'l aş-ĥābi min ghayri'ĥtimāli	وَلِلصِّدِّيقِ رُجْحَانٌ جَلِيٌّ عَلَى الْأَصْحَابِ مِنْ غَيْرِ احْتِمَالِ
36	wa li'l fārūqi rujĥān^{un} wa fađl^{un} álā úthmāna dhi'n nūrayni áālī	وَلِلْفَارُوقِ رُجْحَانٌ وَفَضْلٌ عَلَى عُثْمَانَ ذِي النُّورَيْنِ عَالِي
37	wa dhu'n nūrayni ĥaqqa^{n} kāna khayra^{n} mina'l karrāri fī şaffi'l qitāli	وَذُو النُّورَيْنِ حَقًّا كَانَ خَيْرًا مِنَ الْكَرَّارِ فِي صَفِّ الْقِتَالِ
38	wa li'l karrāri fađl^{un} baáda hādha ála'l aghyāri ţurra^{n} lā tubālī	وَلِلْكَرَّارِ فَضْلٌ بَعْدَ هَذَا عَلَى الْأَغْيَارِ طُرًّا لَا تُبَالِي
39	wa li'ş şiddīqati'l rujĥānu faálam ála'z zahrā'yi fī baáđi'l khilāli	وَلِلصِّدِّيقَةِ الرُّجْحَانُ فَاعْلَمْ عَلَى الزَّهْرَاءِ فِي بَعْضِ الْخِلَالِ

40	wa lam yalán yazīda^{n} báda mawt^{in} siwa'l mikthāri fi'l ighrāyi ghālī	وَلَـمْ يَلْعَنْ يَزِيْداً بَعْدَ مَوْتٍ سِوَى الْمِكْثَارِ فِي الإِغْرَاءِ غَـالِي
41	wa īmānu'l muqallidi dhū iýtibār^{in} bi anwāýi'd dalāyili ka'n nişāli	وَإِيْمَـانُ الْمُقَلِّـدِ ذُو اعْتِبَارٍ بِأَنْوَاعِ الدَّلَائِلِ كَالنِّصَالِ
42	wa mā udhr^{un} li dhī áql^{in} bi jahl^{in} bi khallāqi'l asāfili wa'l a-áālī	وَمَـا عُذْرٌ لِـذِي عَقْلٍ بِجَهْلٍ بِخَـلَّاقِ الأَسَافِلِ وَالأَعَالِي
43	wa mā īmānu shakhş^{in} ĥāla ba's^{in} bi maqbūl^{in} li faqdi'l imtithāli	وَمَا إِيمَانُ شَخْصٍ حَـالَ بَأْسٍ بِمَقْبُولٍ لِـفَقْدِ الإِمْتِثَالِ
44	wa mā afáālu khayr^{in} fī ĥisāb^{in} mina'l īmāni mafrūđa'l wişāli	وَمَـا أَفْعَـالُ خَيْرٍ فِي حِسَابٍ مِنَ الإِيْمَانِ مَفْرُوْضَ الْوِصَالِ
45	wa lā yuqđā bi kufr^{in} wa'rtidād^{in} bi áhr^{in} aw bi qatl^{in} wa'khtizāli	وَلَا يُقْضَى بِكُفْرٍ وَارْتِـدَادٍ بِعَـهْرٍ أَوْ بِـقَتْلٍ وَاخْتِزَالِ
46	wa man yanwi'rtidāda^{n} báada dahr^{in} yaşir án dīni ĥaqq^{in} dha'nsilāli	وَمَنْ يَنْوِ ارْتِدَاداً بَعْـدَ دَهْرٍ يَصِـرْ عَنْ دِيْنِ حَقٍّ ذَا انْسِلَالِ
47	wa lafżu'l kufri min ghayri'ýtiqād^{in} bi ţawý^{in} raddu dīn^{in} bi'ghtifāli	وَلَـفْظُ الْكُفْرِ مِنْ غَيْرِ اعْتِقَادٍ بِطَوْعٍ رَدُّ دِيْنٍ بِـاغْتِفَالِ

48	wa lā yuĥkam bi kufr^{in} ĥāla sukr^{in} bi mā yahdhī wa yalghū bi'rtijāli	وَلَا يُحْكَمْ بِكُفْرٍ حَالَ سُكْرٍ بِمَا يَهْذِي وَيَلْغُو بِارْتِجَالِ
49	wa ma'l mádūmu mar'yiyyan wa shayya^{n} li fiqh^{in} lāĥa fī yumni'l hilāli	وَمَا الْمَعْدُومُ مَرْئِيًّا وَشَيْئًا لِفِقْهٍ لَاحَ فِي يُمْنِ الْهِلَالِ
50	wa ghayrāni'l mukawwanu lā ka shayy^{in} máa't takwīni khudh-hu li'ktiĥāli	وَغَيْرَانِ الْمُكَوَّنُ لَا كَشَيْءٍ مَعَ التَّكْوِينِ خُذْهُ لِاكْتِحَالِ
51	wa inna's suĥta rizq^{un} mithlu ĥill^{in} wa in yakrah maqālī kullu qālī	وَإِنَّ السُّحْتَ رِزْقٌ مِثْلُ حِلٍّ وَإِنْ يَكْرَهْ مَقَالِي كُلُّ قَالِي
52	wa fi'l ajdāthi án tawĥīdi rabbī sa-yublā kullu shakhş^{in} bi's su-āli	وَفِي الْأَجْدَاثِ عَنْ تَوْحِيدِ رَبِّي سَيُبْلَى كُلُّ شَخْصٍ بِالسُّؤَالِ
53	wa li'l kuffāri wa'l fussāqi yuqđā ádhābu'l qabri min sūyi'l fiáāli	وَلِلْكُفَّارِ وَالْفُسَّاقِ يُقْضَى عَذَابُ الْقَبْرِ مِنْ سُوءِ الْفِعَالِ
54	dukhūlu'n nāsi fi'l jannāti fađl^{un} mina'r Raĥmāni yā ahla'l amālī	دُخُولُ النَّاسِ فِي الْجَنَّاتِ فَضْلٌ مِنَ الرَّحْمٰنِ يَا أَهْلَ الْآمَالِ
55	ĥisābu'n nāsi baáda'l baáthi ĥaqq^{un} fa-kūnū bi't taĥarruzi án wabāli	حِسَابُ النَّاسِ بَعْدَ الْبَعْثِ حَقٌّ فَكُونُوا بِالتَّحَرُّزِ عَنْ وَبَالِ

56	wa yuúta'l kutbu baáđa^{n} naĥwa yumnā wa baáđa^{n} naĥwa żahr^{in} wa'sh shimāli	وَيُعطَى الْكُتْبُ بَعْضاً نَحْوَ يُمْنَى وَبَعْضاً نَحْوَ ظَهْرٍ وَالشِّمَالِ
57	wa ĥaqq^{un} waznu a-ámālin wa jar-y^{un} álā matni's şirāţi bilā 'htibālī	وَحَقٌّ وَزْنُ أَعْمَالٍ وَجَرْيٌ عَلَى مَتْنِ الصِّرَاطِ بِلَا اهْتِبَالِ
58	wa marjuww^{un} shafāátu ahli khayr^{in} li aş-ĥābi'l kabāyiri ka'l jibāli	وَمَرْجُوٌّ شَفَاعَةُ أَهْلِ خَيْرٍ لِأَصْحَابِ الْكَبَائِرِ كَالْجِبَالِ
59	wa li'd daáwāti ta'thīr^{un} balīgh^{un} wa qad yanfīhi aş-ĥābu'đ đalāli	وَلِلدَّعْوَاتِ تَأْثِيرٌ بَلِيغٌ وَقَدْ يَنْفِيهِ أَصْحَابُ الضَّلَالِ
60	wa dunyānā ĥadīth^{un} wa'l hayūlā ádīmu'l kawni fa'smaá bi'jtidhāli	وَدُنْيَانَا حَدِيثٌ وَالْهَيُولَى عَدِيمُ الْكَوْنِ فَاسْمَعْ بِاجْتِذَالِ
61	wa li'l jannāti wa'n nīrāni kawn^{un} álayhā marru aĥwāl^{in} khawālī	وَلِلْجَنَّاتِ وَالنِّيرَانِ كَوْنٌ عَلَيْهَا مَرُّ أَحْوَالٍ خَوَالِي
62	wa dhu'l yīmāni lā yabqā muqīma^{n} bi shu-mi'dh dhanbi fī dāri'shtiáāli	وَذُو الْإِيمَانِ لَا يَبْقَى مُقِيماً بِشُؤْمِ الذَّنْبِ فِي دَارِ اشْتِعَالِ
63	laqad albastu li't tawĥīdi nażma^{n} badīý ash-shakli ka's siĥri'l ĥalāli	لَقَدْ أَلْبَسْتُ لِلتَّوْحِيدِ نَظْماً بَدِيعَ الشَّكْلِ كَالسِّحْرِ الْحَلَالِ

64	yusalli’l qalba ka’l bushrā bi rawĥ^{in} wa yuĥyi’r rūĥa ka’l maā’iz zulāli	يُسَلِّي الْقَلْبَ كَالْبُشْرَىٰ بِرَوْحٍ وَيُحْيِي الرُّوحَ كَالْمَاءِ الزُّلَالِ
65	fa khūđū fīhi ĥifża^{n} wa’átiqāda^{n} tanālu jinsa aşnāfi’l manāli	فَخُوضُوا فِيهِ حِفْظاً وَاعْتِقَاداً تَنَالُوا جِنْسَ أَصْنَافِ الْمَنَالِ
66	wa kūnū áwna hādha’l ábdi dahra^{n} bi dhıkri’l khayri fī ĥāli’btihāli	وَكُونُوا عَوْنَ هَذَا الْعَبْدِ دَهْراً بِذِكْرِ الْخَيْرِ فِي حَالِ ابْتِهَالِ
67	laáll’llāha yaáfūhu bi fađl^{in} wa yúţīhi’s sáādata fi’l maāli	لَعَلَّ اللهَ يَعْفُوهُ بِفَضْلٍ وَيُعْطِيهِ السَّعَادَةَ فِي الْمَآلِ
68	wa inni’d dahra adúū kun’ha wusýī li man bi’l khayri yawma^{n} qad dáā lī	وَإِنِّي الدَّهْرَ أَدْعُو كُنْهَ وُسْعِي لِمَنْ بِالْخَيْرِ يَوْماً قَدْ دَعَا لِي

Appendix B

QUR'ĀNIC VERSES

These are the Qur'ānic verses mentioned in translation in footnotes. In all instances, the translation is cited first and the text is below it.

Footnote #11

He is not Pleased for His slaves to disbelieve [Zumar 39:7].

وَلَا يَرۡضَىٰ لِعِبَادِهِ ٱلۡكُفۡرَۖ

Footnote #16

Ask them: 'Whose witness is the greatest?' Say: Allāh is the [greatest] Witness between I and you [Anáām, 6:19].

قُلۡ أَيُّ شَيۡءٍ أَكۡبَرُ شَهَٰدَةٗۖ قُلِ ٱللَّهُۖ شَهِيدُۢ بَيۡنِي وَبَيۡنَكُمۡۚ

Footnote #19

Glorify the Name of your Lord [Al-Aálā, v1].

سَبِّحِ ٱسۡمَ رَبِّكَ ٱلۡأَعۡلَى

Footnote #24

And disbelievers will never cease doubting, until the Final Hour comes upon them suddenly, or comes punishment, on that day which will be fruitless for them [Ĥajj 22:55].

وَلَا يَزَالُ ٱلَّذِينَ كَفَرُواْ فِي مِرۡيَةٖ مِّنۡهُ حَتَّىٰ
تَأۡتِيَهُمُ ٱلسَّاعَةُ بَغۡتَةً أَوۡ يَأۡتِيَهُمۡ عَذَابُ يَوۡمٍ عَقِيمٍ

And when you said: "O Mūsā, we will certainly not believe you until we see Allāh openly [with our own eyes]" [Baqarah, 2:55].

وَإِذْ قُلْتُمْ يَٰمُوسَىٰ لَن نُّؤْمِنَ لَكَ حَتَّىٰ نَرَى ٱللَّهَ جَهْرَةً

The People of the Book ask you to cause a book to descend upon them from the heavens. Indeed, they have asked Mūsā for something even greater than this, when they said: 'Show us Allāh manifestly.' They were struck by a thunderbolt for their transgression. [Nisā'a, 4:153]

يَسْـَٔلُكَ أَهْلُ ٱلْكِتَٰبِ أَن تُنَزِّلَ عَلَيْهِمْ كِتَٰبًا مِّنَ ٱلسَّمَآءِ ۚ فَقَدْ سَأَلُوا۟

مُوسَىٰٓ أَكْبَرَ مِن ذَٰلِكَ فَقَالُوٓا۟ أَرِنَا ٱللَّهَ جَهْرَةً فَأَخَذَتْهُمُ ٱلصَّٰعِقَةُ بِظُلْمِهِمْ ۚ

When our signs [Qur'ānic verses] are recited to them, they say: 'These are naught, but legends of ancient folk' [Qalam, 68:15].

إِذَا تُتْلَىٰ عَلَيْهِ ءَايَٰتُنَا قَالَ أَسَٰطِيرُ ٱلْأَوَّلِينَ

Indeed, there is nothing else except our death for just once; and we shall not be resurrected. Bring forth our forefathers if you are indeed truthful. [Dukhān, 44:35-36].

إِنْ هِىَ إِلَّا مَوْتَتُنَا ٱلْأُولَىٰ وَمَا نَحْنُ بِمُنشَرِينَ ۞ فَأْتُوا۟ بِـَٔابَآئِنَآ إِن كُنتُمْ صَٰدِقِينَ ۞

When he comes to know of our signs [Qur'ānic verses] he takes to mockery... [Jāthiyah, 45:9].

وَإِذَا عَلِمَ مِنْ ءَايَٰتِنَا شَيْـًٔا ٱتَّخَذَهَا هُزُوًا ۚ

Death will come to you, even if you take shelter in the most formidable fortress...[Nisā'a, 4:78].

أَيۡنَمَا تَكُونُواْ يُدۡرِككُّمُ ٱلۡمَوۡتُ وَلَوۡ كُنتُمۡ فِي بُرُوجٖ مُّشَيَّدَةٖۗ

Until death comes to them, and they will say: "O our Lord, send us back" [Mu'minūn, 23:99].

حَتَّىٰٓ إِذَا جَآءَ أَحَدَهُمُ ٱلۡمَوۡتُ قَالَ رَبِّ ٱرۡجِعُونِ

If only you could see the Angels yank the souls of disbelievers, and slap their faces and strike their backs, [saying:] 'Now, taste the punishment of the scorching fire' [Anfāl, 8:50].

وَلَوۡ تَرَىٰٓ إِذۡ يَتَوَفَّى ٱلَّذِينَ كَفَرُواْ ٱلۡمَلَٰٓئِكَةُ يَضۡرِبُونَ
وُجُوهَهُمۡ وَأَدۡبَٰرَهُمۡ وَذُوقُواْ عَذَابَ ٱلۡحَرِيقِ

Be lenient with disbelievers and give them some time. [Ṭāriq, 86:17].

فَمَهِّلِ ٱلۡكَٰفِرِينَ أَمۡهِلۡهُمۡ رُوَيۡدَۢا

Do wait; indeed, we too are waiting. [Hūd, 11:122].

وَٱنتَظِرُوٓاْ إِنَّا مُنتَظِرُونَ

Footnote #27
And He is Omnipotent over His slaves. [Sūrah Anáām, 6:18]

وَهُوَ ٱلۡقَاهِرُ فَوۡقَ عِبَادِهِۦۚ

Raĥmān made istiwā'a on the Throne. [Sūrah Ṭā-Hā, 20:5]

ٱلرَّحۡمَٰنُ عَلَى ٱلۡعَرۡشِ ٱسۡتَوَىٰ

Footnote #31

Wheresover you turn, you will find the Mercy of Allāh facing you [Baqarah, 2:115].

فَأَيْنَمَا تُوَلُّوا۟ فَثَمَّ وَجْهُ ٱللَّهِ

There is nothing like Him [Shūrā, 42:11].

لَيْسَ كَمِثْلِهِۦ شَىْءٌ

Footnote #33

The Lord of the Day of Recompense. [Fātiĥah, 1:4].

مَـٰلِكِ يَوْمِ ٱلدِّينِ

Footnote #38

And that Exalted is our Lord Sustainer; He has not taken [unto himself] a wife or a son. [Jinn 72:3]

وَأَنَّهُۥ تَعَـٰلَىٰ جَدُّ رَبِّنَا مَا ٱتَّخَذَ صَـٰحِبَةً وَلَا وَلَدًا

Footnote #40.

Every soul shall taste death. [Aāl Ímrān, 3:185].

كُلُّ نَفْسٍ ذَآئِقَةُ ٱلْمَوْتِ

Footnote #41.

Whose dominion is it this day? [Everything] belongs to Allāh, the One, the Absolute Subduer [Ghāfir, 40:16].

لِّمَنِ ٱلْمُلْكُ ٱلْيَوْمَ لِلَّهِ ٱلْوَٰحِدِ ٱلْقَهَّارِ

There is nothing else except for our life in this world, we die and we live; and we shall not be resurrected. [Mu'minūn, 23:37].

إِنْ هِىَ إِلَّا حَيَاتُنَا ٱلدُّنْيَا نَمُوتُ وَنَحْيَا وَمَا نَحْنُ بِمَبْعُوثِينَ

And they say, there is nothing [else] except this life of ours in this world; we die and we live and it is only time that wastes us away. They do not speak from knowledge – it is merely their conjecture [Jāthiyah, 45:24].

وَقَالُوا۟ مَا هِىَ إِلَّا حَيَاتُنَا ٱلدُّنْيَا نَمُوتُ وَنَحْيَا وَمَا يُهْلِكُنَآ إِلَّا ٱلدَّهْرُ ۚ وَمَا لَهُم بِذَٰلِكَ مِنْ عِلْمٍ ۖ إِنْ هُمْ إِلَّا يَظُنُّونَ

Every soul shall taste death. You will be given your full recompense only on the Day of Resurrection. Whosoever is saved from Fire and made to enter Paradise [on that day] has truly succeeded. The life of this world is nothing but a materialistic delusion [Aāl Ímrān, 3:185].

كُلُّ نَفْسٍ ذَآئِقَةُ ٱلْمَوْتِ ۗ وَإِنَّمَا تُوَفَّوْنَ أُجُورَكُمْ يَوْمَ ٱلْقِيَـٰمَةِ ۖ

فَمَن زُحْزِحَ عَنِ ٱلنَّارِ وَأُدْخِلَ ٱلْجَنَّةَ فَقَدْ فَازَ ۗ وَمَا ٱلْحَيَوٰةُ ٱلدُّنْيَآ إِلَّا مَتَـٰعُ ٱلْغُرُورِ

Footnote #42

Indeed, We have revealed this Qur'ān and We shall Protect it. [Ĥijr 15:9].

إِنَّا نَحْنُ نَزَّلْنَا ٱلذِّكْرَ وَإِنَّا لَهُۥ لَحَـٰفِظُونَ

Footnote #43

No soul knoweth what is hidden for them; among things extremely pleasing to the eyes, as a reward of their deeds [Sajdah, 32:17].

فَلَا تَعْلَمُ نَفْسٌ مَّآ أُخْفِىَ لَهُم مِّن قُرَّةِ أَعْيُنٍ جَزَآءًۢ بِمَا كَانُوا۟ يَعْمَلُونَ

Footnote #44

Indeed, the hypocrites are in the lowest depths of hellfire [Nisā'a, 4:145].

إِنَّ ٱلْمُنَٰفِقِينَ فِى ٱلدَّرْكِ ٱلْأَسْفَلِ مِنَ ٱلنَّارِ

Footnote #45

Indeed Allāh has damned the disbelievers and has prepared for them a blaze. They shall stay in it forever [Aĥzāb 33:64-65].

إِنَّ ٱللَّهَ لَعَنَ ٱلْكَٰفِرِينَ وَأَعَدَّ لَهُمْ سَعِيرًا ۝ خَٰلِدِينَ فِيهَآ أَبَدًا

Footnote #52

He lets go astray whom He wills, and He guides whom he Wills [Naĥl, 16:93].

وَلَٰكِن يُضِلُّ مَن يَشَآءُ وَيَهْدِى مَن يَشَآءُ

Footnote #56

Rather, he is the Messenger of Allāh and he is the Seal of all Prophets [Aĥzāb, 33:40]

وَلَٰكِن رَّسُولَ ٱللَّهِ وَخَاتَمَ ٱلنَّبِيِّـۧنَ

Footnote #60

We have not sent thee, except as a mercy to the universe. [Anbiyā'a, 21:107].

وَمَآ أَرْسَلْنَٰكَ إِلَّا رَحْمَةً لِّلْعَٰلَمِينَ

Footnote #64

Glory to Him, who took His slave on a journey from the Masjid al-Ĥarām to the Farthest Mosque [Masjid al-Aqṣā, Jerusalem] in a portion of the night...[Al-Isrā'a, 17:1]

سُبْحَٰنَ ٱلَّذِىٓ أَسْرَىٰ بِعَبْدِهِۦ لَيْلًا مِّنَ ٱلْمَسْجِدِ ٱلْحَرَامِ إِلَى ٱلْمَسْجِدِ ٱلْأَقْصَا

Footnote #72

And We have not sent forth [a Messenger] before you, except men [Anbiyā'a, 21:7].

وَمَآ أَرۡسَلۡنَا قَبۡلَكَ إِلَّا رِجَالٗا نُّوحِيٓ إِلَيۡهِمۡۖ

Footnote #82

Allāh Knows well, whither to place His Message [Anáām, 6:124].

ٱللَّهُ أَعۡلَمُ حَيۡثُ يَجۡعَلُ رِسَالَتَهُۥۗ

Footnote #97

But their [accepting] faith did not benefit them, when they saw Our punishment...[Ghāfir, 40:85].

فَلَمۡ يَكُ يَنفَعُهُمۡ إِيمَٰنُهُمۡ لَمَّا رَأَوۡاْ بَأۡسَنَاۖ

And repentance is not [accepted] from those who keep sinning until death comes to them; and one of them says [at the time of death,] 'I repent now', or of those who die as disbelievers...[Nisā'a, 4:18].

وَلَيۡسَتِ ٱلتَّوۡبَةُ لِلَّذِينَ يَعۡمَلُونَ ٱلسَّيِّـَٔاتِ حَتَّىٰٓ إِذَا حَضَرَ أَحَدَهُمُ ٱلۡمَوۡتُ
قَالَ إِنِّي تُبۡتُ ٱلۡـَٰٔنَ وَلَا ٱلَّذِينَ يَمُوتُونَ وَهُمۡ كُفَّارٌۚ

Footnote #104

Whoever disbelieves in Allāh after having believed in Him – except who is under compulsion while his heart is at peace concerning Islām; but the one who disbelieved with an open-heart, upon him is the Wrath of Allāh and for them [disbelievers] is a great punishment. [Naĥl 16:106].

مَن كَفَرَ بِٱللَّهِ مِنۢ بَعۡدِ إِيمَٰنِهِۦٓ إِلَّا مَنۡ أُكۡرِهَ وَقَلۡبُهُۥ مُطۡمَئِنُّۢ بِٱلۡإِيمَٰنِ
وَلَٰكِن مَّن شَرَحَ بِٱلۡكُفۡرِ صَدۡرٗا فَعَلَيۡهِمۡ غَضَبٞ مِّنَ ٱللَّهِ وَلَهُمۡ عَذَابٌ عَظِيمٞ

Footnote #110

And I created you, prior to which you were nothing [Maryam, 19:9].

وَقَدْ خَلَقْتُكَ مِن قَبْلُ وَلَمْ تَكُ شَيْـًٔا

Indeed, there has passed a time upon the human, when he was not even a thing mentioned anywhere [Insān, 76:1].

هَلْ أَتَىٰ عَلَى ٱلْإِنسَٰنِ حِينٌ مِّنَ ٱلدَّهْرِ لَمْ يَكُن شَيْـًٔا مَّذْكُورًا

Indeed, the tremor of the Final Hour is a terrible thing [Ĥajj, 22:1].

إِنَّ زَلْزَلَةَ ٱلسَّاعَةِ شَىْءٌ عَظِيمٌ

Footnote #115

Indeed, Our saying to a thing, when We Will for it [to exist], that We say 'Be' and it becomes [Naĥl, 16:40].

إِنَّمَا قَوْلُنَا لِشَىْءٍ إِذَآ أَرَدْنَٰهُ أَن نَّقُولَ لَهُۥ كُن فَيَكُونُ

He has Power over all things [Baqarah, 2:20]

إِنَّ ٱللَّهَ عَلَىٰ كُلِّ شَىْءٍ قَدِيرٌ

He is the Creator of every thing [Anáām, 6:101].

وَخَلَقَ كُلَّ شَىْءٍ

He is the Creator of every thing [Anáām, 6:102].

خَٰلِقُ كُلِّ شَىْءٍ فَٱعْبُدُوهُ

Footnote #121

Enter paradise for the [good] deeds you used to do [Naĥl, 16:32].

ٱدْخُلُوا۟ ٱلْجَنَّةَ بِمَا كُنتُمْ تَعْمَلُونَ

Footnote #125

Soon his account shall be taken, and [he will be] accounted in an easy manner [Inshiqāq, 84:8].

فَسَوْفَ يُحَاسَبُ حِسَابًا يَسِيرًا

Read [aloud] your record; you suffice [for yourself] on this day to take the account of your own self [Isrā'a, 17:14].

ٱقْرَأْ كِتَٰبَكَ كَفَىٰ بِنَفْسِكَ ٱلْيَوْمَ عَلَيْكَ حَسِيبًا

Footnote #129

As for him, whose book of deeds is given in his right hand; soon his account shall be taken, and [he shall be] accounted in an easy manner; and he shall return to his family in happiness; as for him, whose book of deeds is given behind his back; soon he shall cry out for extermination; [but] he will be sent into a blazing fire [Inshiqāq, 84:7-11].

فَأَمَّا مَنْ أُوتِىَ كِتَٰبَهُۥ بِيَمِينِهِۦ ۞ فَسَوْفَ يُحَاسَبُ حِسَابًا يَسِيرًا ۞ وَيَنقَلِبُ إِلَىٰٓ أَهْلِهِۦ مَسْرُورًا

وَأَمَّا مَنْ أُوتِىَ كِتَٰبَهُۥ وَرَآءَ ظَهْرِهِۦ ۞ فَسَوْفَ يَدْعُوا۟ ثُبُورًا ۞ وَيَصْلَىٰ سَعِيرًا ۞

As for him, who is given his book of deeds in his left hand, he will say 'Alas! Were it that my book of deeds had never been given to me and were it that I knew nothing of my account' [Ĥāqqah, 69:25-26].

وَأَمَّا مَنْ أُوتِىَ كِتَٰبَهُۥ بِشِمَالِهِۦ فَيَقُولُ يَٰلَيْتَنِى لَمْ أُوتَ كِتَٰبِيَهْ ۞ وَلَمْ أَدْرِ مَا حِسَابِيَهْ

Footnote #130

And the Weighing [of deeds] on that day is true. They, whose scales are heavy are indeed the successful ones. And they, whose scales are meagre are the ones who have put their own selves into peril and a loss – recompense for their unjust rejection of Our signs [Aárāf, 7:8-9].

وَٱلْوَزْنُ يَوْمَئِذٍ ٱلْحَقُّ ۚ فَمَن ثَقُلَتْ مَوَٰزِينُهُۥ فَأُو۟لَـٰٓئِكَ هُمُ ٱلْمُفْلِحُونَ ۞

وَمَنْ خَفَّتْ مَوَٰزِينُهُۥ فَأُو۟لَـٰٓئِكَ ٱلَّذِينَ خَسِرُوٓا۟ أَنفُسَهُم بِمَا كَانُوا۟ بِـَٔايَـٰتِنَا يَظْلِمُونَ

And We shall place the Scales of Justice on the Day of Resurrection... [Anbiyā'a, 21:47].

وَنَضَعُ ٱلْمَوَٰزِينَ ٱلْقِسْطَ لِيَوْمِ ٱلْقِيَـٰمَةِ

Footnote #131

And there is none among you, except that he will have to cross [the bridge] upon hell [Maryam, 19:71].

وَإِن مِّنكُمْ إِلَّا وَارِدُهَا ۚ

Footnote #132

Nigh it is, that your Lord Sustainer will bring you forth upon the Extolled Station [Isrā'a, 17:79].

عَسَىٰٓ أَن يَبْعَثَكَ رَبُّكَ مَقَامًا مَّحْمُودًا

Footnote #133

Indeed, Allāh will not forgive that partners be ascribed to him [or commit kufr]; but may forgive anything besides, for whomsoever He Wills. [Nisā'a, 4:48].

إِنَّ ٱللَّهَ لَا يَغْفِرُ أَن يُشْرَكَ بِهِۦ وَيَغْفِرُ مَا دُونَ ذَٰلِكَ لِمَن يَشَآءُ ۚ

Footnote #134

Call upon Me; I will Answer your (prayers) [Ghāfir, 40:60].

وَقَالَ رَبُّكُمُ ٱدۡعُونِيٓ أَسۡتَجِبۡ لَكُمۡۚ

Footnote #141

[*Paradise is already*] *prepared for the pious* [Aāl Ímrān, 3:133].

أُعِدَّتۡ لِلۡمُتَّقِينَ

[*Hell is already*] *prepared for the disbelievers* [Baqarah, 2:24].

أُعِدَّتۡ لِلۡكَٰفِرِينَ

They shall abide in it forever [Nisā'a, 4:57].

خَٰلِدِينَ فِيهَآ أَبَدٗاۖ

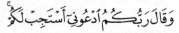

Appendix C

TRANSLITERATION KEY

Arabic Letter	Latin Character	Arabic Example	Transliteration	Similar Sound
ا أ ء	a	أمير	**a**mīr	**a**mazing
ب	b	باب	**b**āb	**b**asket
ت ة	t	تاج	**t**āj	**t** in French **t**rois
ث	th	ثابت	**th**ābit	**th**ing
ج	j	جسد	**j**asad	**j**am
ح	ĥ	حسن	**ĥ**asan	similar to **h**ose no English equivalent voiceless pharyngeal fricative
خ	kh	خبر	**kh**abar	similar to Scottish lo**ch** no english equivalent
د	d	دار	**d**ār	**d** in French **d**ais
ذ	dh	ذكر	**dh**ikr	**th**ere
ر	r	راشد	**r**āshid	trilled **r** as in **r**ose
ز	z	زكي	**z**akī	**z**ebra
س	s	سهل	**s**ahl	**s**olid
ش	sh	شاب	**sh**āb	**sh**ock
ص	ş	صبر	**ş**abr	pharyngeal **s** no English equivalent
ض	đ	ضياء	**đ**iyā'a	similar to **d**aughter no English equivalent
ط	ţ	طب	**ţ**ibb	pharyngeal **t** no English equivalent
ظ	ż	ظل	**ż**ill	pharyngeal **z** no English equivalent

Arabic Letter	Latin Character	Arabic Example	Transliteration	Similar Sound
ع	á, í, ú, ý	عرب علم عمر عيد	**á**rab **í**lm **ú**mar **ý**īd	voiced pharyngeal fricative no English equivalent
غ	gh	غار	**gh**ār	as in French **r** **r**ester voiced uvular fricative
ف	f	فجر	**f**ajr	**f**lower
ق	q	قريب	**q**arīb	a guttural **k** voiceless uvular stop no English equivalent
ك	k	كتاب	**k**itāb	**k**in
ل	l	لباس	**l**ibās	**l**ate
م	m	مال	**m**āl	**m**orning
ن	n	نور	**n**ūr	**n**oon
ه	h	هدى	**h**udā	**h**ouse
و	w	وزير	**w**azīr	**w**ord
ي	y	يد	**y**ad	**y**ellow
إ	i	إدام	**i**dām	**i**nsight
أ	a	أتم	**a**tam	**a**dvent
ا	ā	باب	b**ā**b	f**a**ther
ي	ī	سرير	sar**ī**r	tr**ee**
و	ū	طور	ṭ**ū**r	r**oo**t
عا	áā	عالم	**áā**lim	-

Arabic Letter	Latin Character	Arabic Example	Transliteration	Similar Sound
عي	ýī	عيد	**ýī**d	-
عو	úū	عود	**úū**d	-
شّ	sh'sh sh-sh	الشمس	ash'shams ash-shams	-
أ	a' or a-	مأمور	ma'mūr	-
ئ	i'y or i-y	بئس	bi'ysa bi-ysa	-
ؤ	u' or u-	لؤلؤ سؤلك	lu'lu' su-lika	-
	'	أصحاب تكحيل أسهل	aş'ĥāb tak'ĥīl as'hal	separator to distinguish between sounds represented by letter pairs
	-	أصحاب تكحيل أسهل	aş-ĥāb tak-ĥīl as-hal	separator to distinguish between sounds represented by letter pairs
	superscript	من	mi^n	to indicate an elision
	-	مآرب	ma-ārib	separator when elongation follows a vowel

In transliteration of Arabic names, the definite article **'al'** is not transcribed *always* for readability, even though it may be incorrect in the original. The following rules are followed:

a. The 'al' is retained when used as an auxiliary, as in Abu Bakr **al**-Bayhaqī and Badruddīn **al**-Áynī.

b. It is omitted when used alone, as in Bayhaqi or Áynī.

c. It is retained when the full name of the book is transcribed, but omitted when the book is known by its popular name like *Durr al-Mukhtār*.

SOURCES

This translation is based on the the sources mentioned below. I have referred to various commentaries and annotations for clarifications found in footnotes.

1. ***Bad'a al-Amālī, et al:*** An anthology of four classical texts – *Jawharah al-Tawĥīd, Bad' al-Amālī, Bayqūnīyyah* and *Raĥbiyyah.* Annotated by Ábd al-Salām Shākir and reviewed by Shaykh Adīb al-Kallās, published by Dār Iqra'a, Damascus, 2001.

2. ***Đaw al-Máālī li Badyi'l Amālī***: The well-known commentary of Mawlānā Álī al-Qārī; published in Istanbul in the year 1319 AH by Ĥusayn Ĥilmī al-Katbi, 48 pages.

3. ***Đaw al-Máālī li Badyi'l Amālī***: Álī al-Qārī, annotated by Ábd al-Salām Shannār; published by Dār al-Bayrūtī, Damascus, 2005.

4. ***Đaw al-Máālī li Badyi'l Amālī***: Álī al-Qārī, edited by Muĥammad Ádnān Darwīsh, published by Dār Iqra'a, Damascus, 2002.

5. ***Daraj al-Máālī Sharĥ Bad' al-Amālī*:** The commentary of Ízzuddīn Ibn Jamāáh [d. 819 AH], Mu'assasah al-Kutub al-Thaqafiyah, Tripoli, Lebanon, 2011.

6. ***Daraj al-Máālī Sharĥ Bad' al-Amālī*:** Manuscript of the above from King Saud University #7381, dated around 12 century Hijri.

7. ***Daw al-Máālī and Mukhtaşar Sharĥ Bakrī***: Both commentaries in the same volume, published by Dar Bayrūtī, 2011; edited by Khaldūn Álī Zaynuddīn.

8. ***Jāmiý al-La'ālī Sharĥ Bad'il Amālī:*** A modern commentary by Qāđī Shaykh Muĥammad Aĥmad Kanáān, Lebanon. He completed the commentary in the year 2008 (as mentioned in the conclusion). Published by Dār al-Bashāyir al-Islāmiyyah, 2010.

9. ***Nukhbatu'l La'ālī*** - Shaykh Muĥammad ibn Sulaymān al-Ĥalabī al-Rayĥāwī [d. 1228 AH]. Published in Turkey and reprinted by Hakikat Kitabevi, 1996.

Note: This translation is based on the words and reading affirmed by Mawlānā Álī al-Qārī in his *Đaw al-Máālī.*

ABOUT THE AUTHOR

Imām Sirājuddīn Abu'l Ĥasan Álī ibn Úthmān ibn Muĥammad ibn Sulaymān al-Taymiyy al-Farghānī al-Uūshī al-Ĥanafī ﷺ: Little is known about him except that he is the author of the poem on Sunni creed famously known as *Bad' al-Amālī*. The author of *Jawāhir al-Mudīyyah*, says that he is the famous author of the *qaşīdah* on áqīdah composed in 66 couplets. Nothing much is known about him. It is said that he passed away during the plague of 575 AH (1179 CE). The following books are attributed to him:[149]

1. *Thawāqib al-Akhbār*

2. *Ghurar al-Akhbār wa Durar al-Ash-áār* (A work concerning certain words mentioned in the ĥadīth of the Prophet ﷺ)

3. *Mashāriq al-Anwār Sharĥ Nişāb al-Akhbār*

4. *Yawāqīt al-Akhbār*

5. The ode: *Bad' al-Amālī* on Sunni creed.

༺༻

Historical Perspective: Imām Uūshī is a contemporary of Ghawth al-Aáżam Sayyid Ábd al-Qadir Jilānī [d. 561 AH]. Among Ĥanafīs, he is a contemporary of Imām Abu'l Ĥasan Álī al-Marghīnānī [d. 593 AH], the author of *Hidāyah*; Imām Ĥusayn ibn Manşūr al-Farghāni Qādī Khān [d. 592 AH] and Imām Álāuddīn Abū Bakr ibn Masúūd al-Kāsānī [d. 587 AH], the author of *Badāyiý al-Şanāyiý*. Chronologically, this text comes

---

[149] Ábd al-Salām Shannār's preface: *Hadiyyah al-Áārifīn*, 1/700; Zirkily in *Aálām*, 4/310.

after the famous *Áqīdah al-Nasafiyyah,* which was written by Imām Úmar ibn Muĥammad an-Nasafi [d. 538 AH] and appears to be the versification of this text. This poem was completed in the year 569 AH.[150]

***Commentaries*:**

1. ***Đaw al-Máālī*** – Mullā Álī al-Qārī [d. 1014 AH]. It is the best known and the most commonly available commentary of the poem. Dār al-Bayrūtī has published it separately with annotations of Shaykh Ábd al-Salām Shannār. Recently a second edition, with footnotes of Shaykh Khaldūn Álī Zaynuddīn has been published [2011] along with commentary of Al-Bakri.

2. ***Daraj al-Máālī*** – Imām Ízzuddīn Muĥammad ibn Jamāáh al-Shāfiýī [d. 819 AH] edited and annotated by Majdī Ghassān Márūf.

3. ***Al-La'ālī fi Sharĥ al-Amālī (Mukhtaşar Sharĥ al-Bakri)*** – Rađiyuddīn Abu'l Qāsim ibn Ĥusayn al Bakrī [passed away around 1121 AH]. Published by Dār al-Bayrūtī.

4. ***Sharĥ Qaşīdah Bad'a al-Amālī*** – Shaykh Nūr Muĥammad ibn Ábd al-Raĥīm al-Lāhorī [d. 1157 AH]. Published by Dr. Khāliq Dād Mālik, HoD of Arabic Department, University of Punjab, Pakistan. It is published by University of Punjab, during the academic year 2003-2005.

---

[150] Yamanī as mentioned in *Ţabaqāt al-Ĥanafiyyah*; *Kashf al-Żunūn*, 2/1350.

5. ***Nukhbatu'l La'ālī*** - Shaykh Muĥammad ibn Sulaymān al-Ĥalabī al-Rayĥāwī [d. 1228 AH]. Published in Turkey and reprinted by Hakikat Kitabevi, 1996.

6. ***Tuĥfat al-A'áālī Hashiyah Đaw al-Máālī*** – A supercommentary on Qārī's commentary by an unknown author.

7. ***Jāmiý al-La'ālī*** - A modern commentary on the poem by Shaykh Muĥammad Aĥmad Kanáān of Lebanon. In this commentary, the author has rearranged the lines of the poem according to topics.

Haji Khalīfah has mentioned[151] the names of some more commentaries:

8. ***Hidāyah Mina'l Iýtiqād li Kathrati Nafýihī Bayn al-Íbād*** – Commentary of Muĥammad ibn Abū Bakr al-Rāzī, which he completed in 751 AH.

9. Commentary of Shaykh Shamsuddīn Muĥammad al-Niksārī [d. 901 AH].

10. ***Nafīs al-Riyāđ li Iýdāmi'l Amrāđ*** – Brief commentary by Shaykh Khalīl ibn al-Álā'a al-Najārī al-Yamanī [d. 632 AH].

11. Commentary of Shaykh Muĥammad ibn Aĥmad ibn Úmar al-Anţākī al-Ĥanafī.

---

[151] *Kashf al-Żunūn*, 2/1350.

Majdī Ghassān, in the preface of *Daraj al-Máālī* mentions the following commentaries:

12. ***Maţlaá al-Mithāl fi'l Áqāýid al-Islamiyyah wa Manbá al-Kamāl fi'l Masāyil al-Kalāmiyyah*** - Imām Ízzuddīn Muĥammad ibn Jamāáh al-Shāfiýī [d. 819 AH].

13. ***Úqūd al-La'ālī*** – Muĥammad al-Nīsābūrī.

14. ***Nashr al-La'ālī*** – Tūnusī al-Ĥanafī.

15. ***Nūr al-Máālī*** – Ibn al-Kātib al-Yankajriyyah al-Yāzijī

16. ***Daw al-La'ālī*** – Supercommentary on the commentary of Yāzijī.

17. ***Sharĥ Bad'a al-Amālī*** by Mir'áshī.

18. ***Sharĥ Bad'a al-Amālī*** by Aydanī.

ABOUT THE TRANSLATOR

Abu Hasan is a student of Islamic sciences and the Sacred Law. He follows the Ĥanafī–Māturīdī madh'hab and is an aspirant to the Qādirī path; he is also an ardent admirer and follower of Alahazrat Imām Aĥmad Riđā Khān al-Baraylawī ﷺ. Abu Hasan translates short works and excerpts for his own edification and shares them for the benefit of students and beginners like himself. Some of his articles can be found on *www.tanwir.org* and *www.ridawi.org*.

RIDAWI
رضا
PRESS

Printed in Great Britain
by Amazon

56342068R00046